Change of Use

Change of Use

Pamela Cunnington

Alphabooks · A & C Black, London

First published 1988 by
Alphabooks Ltd, Sherborne, Dorset
A subsidiary of
A & C Black (Publishers) Ltd
35 Bedford Row, London WC1

ISBN 0 7136 3020 5

British Library Cataloguing in Publication Data

Cunnington, Pamela
  Change of use.
    1. Buildings. Conversion
    I. Title
    690'.24

ISBN 0–7136–3020–5

*The title page shows a converted
windmill between Shepshed and Ashby
near Loughborough.*

Photosetting by Latimer Trend & Company Ltd, Plymouth
Printed by BAS Printers Ltd, Over Wallop, Hampshire, England

Contents

Preface and acknowledgements

The conversion of old buildings may be approached in two ways. In some cases a building considered worthy of preservation is at risk, probably because its original use is no longer viable. Those who wish to see it survive, whether they are individuals, a local society, or the local authority, may see conversion to a new use as a way of saving it, and suggest a number of uses, hoping that a purchaser will come forward. Sometimes, indeed, they will buy the building themselves, either as a holding operation or to carry out a conversion scheme. In other cases the initiative will come from a potential user who is looking for a building, or a site, in a particular area for a particular purpose. He may be interested in saving a good building, but his primary concern will probably be with the economic aspects of the scheme.

In this book I have tried to look at the subject of conversion from both these points of view, and I hope that it will be helpful to owners of problem buildings, to those who are trying to save them, and to potential users. First, I should like to thank all those people who have helped me with information for the book. Mr John Fidler, of the Historic Buildings and Monuments Commission for England, has given me some valuable information about sources of financial aid. The following members of local authority planning departments have given me details of schemes in their areas, and in some cases took time to show me round them: Mr Whimble, of Kent County Council; Mr R.B. Hargreave, of the Metropolitan Borough of Stockport; Mr R.J. Harvey, National Parks Officer, of North Yorkshire County Council; Messrs D. Stenning and J. Boutwood, of Essex County Council; Mr J. Stagg, of Worcester City Council; Mr M. Pearce, of Hampshire County Council; Miss K. Williamson, of the City of London Corporation; Mr T. Pugh, of Lewes Borough Council; Mr A.J. Cook, of the London Borough of Enfield; Mr M. Strawbridge and Mrs Crichton, of Charnwood Borough Council; and Mr A.R. Richardson, of Lichfield District Council.

The following architects have helped me by supplying drawings and photographs of their schemes: Messrs Bodnitz Allan and Partners (Grovelands, Southgate); Messrs Donald Insall and Associates (Hyde Barn, Winchester); Mr P. Lorimer of Messrs Anthony Richardson and Partners (SS. Peter and Paul's Church, Shellow Bowells); Mr Giles Pebody of South Bank Architects (S. James'

Church, Myatts Park); Mr P. Liddiard (S. Peter's Church, Chesil); Mr John Sell of Sell, Wade, Postins (Longcutts Barn, Winfrith Newburgh); Messrs Frederick Burn, Smith and Partners (S. Alban's Church, Wood Street and Pyt House, Tisbury); The Lockside Design Partnership (Lockside Mill, Marple); Messrs M. Drury and G. Steer, of S. Anne's Gate Architects (The Old Chapel, Tollard Royal); Messrs Hinton Brown, Langstone (S. Mary's Centre, Lichfield); Messrs Leonard Manasseh and Partners (Barn at Barnston); Mr C.F. Davies (North Barn, Affpuddle and S. George's Centre, Portland); Messrs Dickinson, Quarme and Associates (The Royal Victoria Patriotic Building, London); Mr P. Lancashire (The Old Candlemakers, Lewes); Mr R. Patterson, Dorset County Architect (Convent of Bethany, Bournemouth); C.H. Design Partnership (The Maltings, and Phillips' Salerooms, Sherborne).

The following building owners have given me permission to describe, and in some cases to include interior photographs of, their buildings: Community Psychiatric Centres, Grovelands, Southgate; Mr and Mrs Thistlethwaite, SS Peter and Paul's Church, Shellow Bowells; Messrs Hunt's Frozen Foods, The Maltings, Sherborne; Messrs Phillips, Auctioneers, Phillips' Salerooms, Sherborne; Interface Church Community, Moulsham Mill, Chelmsford; Mr D. Parker, Berehayes Farm, Whitchurch Canonicorum; Mr Debenham, North Barn, Affpuddle; The Country Houses Association, Pyt House, Tisbury; Mr A. Sanctuary, Bridgeacre, Loders; The East Midlands Housing Association, S. Peter's Court, Mountsorrell; Mrs De Vere Cole, Barn at Odstock; Black Roof Housing Co-op., S. James' Church, Myatts Park. I have also received help and information from Mr T. Robinson of the Countryside Commission, Mr R. Knowles of the Sports Council, Mr M. Corfield of the Kennet and Avon Canal Trust, Mr D. Goodall of the West Country Tourist Board, Mr J. Hamriding of the Council for Small Industries in Rural Areas, Mrs J. Birkett of the Association of Conservation Officers, Messrs Derek Latham and Associates, Mr S. Morris, Mr G. Pitman, and Miss I.Taggart of the Advisory Board for Redundant Churches.

To all these people, and any whom I may inadvertently have omitted, I should like to express my thanks, as their help and co-operation have been of the greatest value to me in writing this book.

The former Green Park railway station, Bath. The old buildings, refurbished, form the entrance to a supermarket and restaurant.

Part I. General principles

1 The historical background

Today we are seeing a considerable interest in converting buildings for new uses. There are, as we shall see later, several reasons for this, and it is important to realise that it is not a new phenomenon. From earliest times there is evidence of buildings having been altered, enlarged and adapted for new or modified uses, provided that the original structure was sufficiently substantial to justify the work involved. This last point is important, and equally relevant today.

Let us start, therefore, by looking back at the history of conversion, to see how, and perhaps why, old buildings have changed their uses in the past. Often the reason was purely economic; it was cheaper to use, and if necessary alter, an existing structure than to start from scratch. Those early men who chose to move into conveniently sited caves rather than put up new hut-like dwellings were showing sound sense, providing themselves with a more substantial shelter as well as saving effort. Still in prehistoric times, but on a grander scale, it might be said that the successive alterations carried out at sites such as Stonehenge were early forms of conversion. While the original purpose of this site cannot be known for certain today, it is clear that its use must have changed sufficiently to justify very substantial remodelling on several occasions.

Coming into the Roman period, there is little evidence of conversion of the native structures, most of which were probably insufficiently substantial to justify such work. At Dorchester, Dorset, however, a neolithic henge monument was altered by the Romans to form an amphitheatre, and this same structure was again altered during the Civil War in the seventeenth century, as part of the town defences. At the end of the Roman period there is some archaeological evidence that the surviving buildings were occupied, and sometimes altered by the native or immigrant people. Indeed, the few Roman structures in Britain which have survived above ground level owe this survival to their having been incorporated in later buildings.

Moving into the medieval period, generally only the more substantial stone buildings—churches, and the houses of the wealthy—would have been considered worth altering and adapting for new uses. The simple timber houses in which most people lived were more likely to have been taken down and rebuilt when they

The historical background

Gatehouse to the Charterhouse, London, incorporated in an eighteenth-century house.

became out of date. Churches were certainly altered, enlarged and adapted to suit not only a growing population, but new and more elaborate forms of worship. In domestic buildings the early Norman castles, with their thick walls and small windows, were often substantially altered and converted to comfortable country houses as more peaceful conditions prevailed.

By the late medieval and Tudor periods even the middle classes, the yeomen and wealthier artisans, were building more substantial houses, of stone, timber or brick, which were worth altering to suit new fashions and technological changes. Insertion of chimney stacks, flooring-over of open halls and enlargement of windows as glass became cheaper, can all be seen in farmhouses and town merchants' houses of this period. The sixteenth century was a time of great changes, religious, political, social and economic. This resulted in a considerable building boom; some of it new, but including a good deal of alteration and conversion work. This can perhaps be seen most clearly in the fate of the monasteries and some other religious buildings. The changes of the Reformation meant that many religious buildings were no longer needed for their original purpose. Large numbers were destroyed, robbed for their materials, but others were altered for a variety of uses. Much of this work was done with little regard for the original design; medieval architecture, as well as medieval churchmanship, was now out of favour. Today, however, we may find these altered buildings attractive and interesting in their own way.

In many cases the monastic church itself was demolished, and the domestic buildings converted, either as one or more secular resi-

ABOVE *The buildings of the Blackfriars, Newcastle-upon-Tyne, now a Heritage Centre, restaurant and craft workshops.* LEFT *The Blackfriars, Hereford, converted to almshouses after the Dissolution.*

dences, or for agricultural or industrial use. In Newcastle-upon-Tyne, the buildings of the former Blackfriars were adapted as halls for the various civic companies. Later, many of these were again converted, to tenements, gradually becoming more and more neglected. After the Second World War the whole complex had become derelict, in danger of demolition, but it has now been given a new lease of life as craft shops, a heritage centre and restaurant (in the former refectory). This case well illustrates the changes that can take place in the lifetime of an old building. Where the monastic church survived, becoming either a cathedral or a parish church, the domestic buildings, designed for a way of life which had ceased to exist, were either demolished or adapted for new uses. In some cases the old communal buildings of the monastery were converted for use by the new secular, often married, clergy; in others they were made to serve a newly established or re-founded school. In Norwich, most of the Church of Saint Helen was converted to an almshouse, while in King's Lynn the Church of Saint James became the town poorhouse, but this has since been demolished. At Cobham in Kent, the secular buildings of the former collegiate church (no longer needed after the college was dissolved and the

Former buildings of Sherborne Abbey, Dorset, incorporated in Sherborne School.

church itself became parochial) were converted into almshouses, a use which survives today.

Most of the monastic buildings were solidly constructed, and for this reason were often retained and converted if required for a new use. If not, they were demolished and their materials used for new buildings. There is little evidence of any effort being made to find suitable uses in order to save good buildings.

Even in parish churches one example of 'conversion' is found at this time. During the later Middle Ages many wealthy families had built chantry chapels in their churches, where they paid for masses and prayers to be said for their souls. Members of the family were generally buried in these chapels, which remained their property even after the chantry foundations had been dissolved and their endowments confiscated after the Reformation. It had become usual, even before this, for the members of the family to sit in its chapel for the public services, partly screened from the rest of the congregation. Now, the altars were removed, but the monuments remained, and the chantry chapel became the family pew, its original purpose probably forgotten after a few generations.

The various changes in urban life in the seventeenth and eighteenth centuries were reflected in town building. In some cases there were areas of complete rebuilding, but often the changes were less drastic. The tendency for wealthy merchants and traders to move out of town centres into the suburbs or the surrounding countryside resulted in their large old houses being divided into tenements, or adapted for commercial or industrial use, their once large gardens being built over for additional tenements or workshops. This process gathered momentum in the later eighteenth

This early nineteenth-century house at Witham, Essex, fell on hard times in the early twentieth century ABOVE, *became a cinema in the 1930s* BELOW, *but is now a public library, as shown* RIGHT. *The original ground floor has been restored.*

RIGHT *A terrace of Georgian houses in Bridge Street, Worcester, had shop fronts inserted in the nineteenth century, but have now reverted to residential use, with the original frontages reinstated, as shown* FAR RIGHT.

A timber-framed hall-house, in Chignall St James, Essex, became a barn but has recently been reconverted as a house.

century, with its agricultural and industrial changes, and a rapid growth in population. In rural areas, too, many buildings found new uses. With changes in farming practice many of the older farmhouses, built in the villages in the days of open-field farming, were replaced by new farm complexes out in the newly enclosed fields. Some of these old houses were divided up into cottages, as were some of the old, now redundant barns in the villages. On the other

This small building in Tamworth, Staffordshire, started as a school in 1820, later became a chapel, and is now a shop.

hand, we sometimes find an old farmhouse downgraded and used as a farm building or store, with a new house built close by.

The increased prosperity of the age also left its mark on the large country houses. Sometimes old Tudor and Stuart houses were remodelled, and their formal gardens replaced by landscaped parks in the latest manner. In other cases, though, a completely new house was built on a different site, the old house either being demolished or converted into tenements, as happened with the Old Manor House, Kingston Maurward, Dorset, when the eighteenth-century house was built some distance away. Incidentally, the Old Manor House is now once more an attractive private residence, while the eighteenth-century house has become an agricultural college.

In the later nineteenth century, still further changes and population growth took place, but now conversion was generally less popular than new building. Both in towns and in the countryside, the prosperity and confidence of the age preferred to express itself in new houses, churches and public buildings wherever there was sufficient money available. Only in poorer towns and villages do we find much evidence of existing buildings being converted and adapted. In our own day there has been a revival of interest in conversion, but often for rather different reasons. We shall look at some of these in the next chapter.

2 Conversion or new build?

We have seen how, and why, buildings were converted in the past. The reasons then were primarily economic; conversion was normally cheaper than new building. A conversion scheme generally uses more labour, and less material than a comparable new building, and until comparatively recently labour costs were low compared with those of materials. Today the position is often reversed; labour costs are higher in relation to those of materials, and the economic arguments in favour of conversion are correspondingly weaker.

Why, then, is there so much interest in conversion today? I think there are a number of reasons which are worth examining, particularly when we are looking into a specific scheme. First, there are the conservation arguments; the desire to preserve good or, perhaps, simply familiar buildings. This is probably due to a widespread public reaction to the wholesale redevelopment of town centres in the 1960s and 1970s. Well known buildings and streets were swept away, and their replacements have not been generally popular. Many buildings which, if not of outstanding merit, were solidly constructed and displayed sound, even fine, craftsmanship gave way to system-built structures which have not always stood the test of

The Holy Jesus Hospital, Newcastle-upon-Tyne, was at one time threatened with demolition for a road scheme. It has, however, been saved and converted to a museum, although its setting has been rather spoiled by the new roads and adjacent buildings.

A former swimming baths in Loughborough has been given a new lease of life as a public hall.

time. The scandalous sight of comparatively recent blocks of flats being blown up because their repair proved uneconomic has given us a greater appreciation of the substantial Victorian terraces they replaced.

Not only houses, but public and other buildings in towns have become accepted as part of our background. While towns have always been subject to change this has generally in the past been a fairly gradual process, giving us time to adjust to one new building before another appeared. The wholesale changes of the past few decades have almost certainly contributed to the current desire to preserve existing buildings. Problems arise when the original uses of the buildings have disappeared. There is then a demand to find a new use to ensure their future survival. This attitude has been encouraged by the Department of the Environment in its circulars, stating that 'new uses are often the key to preservation', and asking local authorities to permit and facilitate such changes.

Partly as a result of this official encouragement, it is often easier to obtain planning permission for a conversion scheme than for a new building. This is especially true in the countryside, where it may be very difficult to obtain permission for a new house in an isolated area unless there is a genuine agricultural need, but where it may be possible to convert an existing barn, mill or other redundant building, if the local authority considers the building to be of sufficient merit and its original use no longer viable. This can create problems. If the building is of real historical or architectural interest, it is clearly best for the original use to continue if at all possible,

17

Conversion or new build?

RIGHT *Cutler Street in the City of London. An interesting combination of new buildings with conversion of old warehouses.*
BELOW *The portico of the old Baptist Chapel, Banbury, was preserved to form the entrance to a supermarket.*

since any conversion scheme, however careful, is almost bound to involve some loss of the original character. On the other hand, if a farmer can obtain planning permission to convert an old barn into a house he will be able to sell it for a much higher price than he could ever hope to obtain for it in agricultural use. There is, therefore, a great temptation for him to maintain that it is no longer viable as a barn; if he is successful, the price he can obtain will probably more than pay for a replacement barn. The problem is a delicate one for the local authority, particularly as the farmer may well be able to erect a new building without the need for planning permission, and simply allow the old barn to decay.

In towns, too, while permission would be refused for certain new buildings on particular sites, a conversion may be allowed if this is the only likely way of preserving buildings of merit, either in their own right or as part of the townscape. This attitude, as well as favouring genuine conversion, can also often result in façade preservation; reconstructing the building completely behind the street frontage. This may be justifiable in certain special cases, but it is not generally to be recommended. Buildings exist, and should be considered, in three dimensions, and their interiors are often as valuable as the exteriors. Preservation of the familiar street picture may be desirable and is likely to win popular approval, but it can result in old streets becoming simply the equivalent of stage sets.

Apart from these considerations which often favour conversion rather than new buildings, there are undoubtedly some people who enjoy the challenge presented by an existing building rather than an open site. Such people are mostly of two types. One group will want to impose their personality on the building, to show what they can do to transform it. The others will want to accept the building for what it is, with its limitations and problems, and be prepared to adapt their way of life accordingly, altering the building as little as possible.

As we have seen, a conversion is not always cheaper than a new building. The cost will depend on the structural condition of the building, and the amount of alteration needed. Before deciding on a conversion scheme, it is advisable to obtain estimated comparative costs of conversion and of a new building of similar size and quality, always bearing in mind that unexpected problems are more likely to arise with a conversion than with a new building. If the cost of conversion is likely to be the greater, this must be considered in conjunction with other factors; the architectural or historic interest of the building, its ultimate financial value, the desirability of the site, and the possibility of finding an equally suitable one for a new building (assuming that demolition would not be permitted).

Once the decision has been made to convert an existing building, there are, as we have seen, two approaches to the problem. If the

A medieval cruck-framed open hall house at Lichfield has been reconstructed as an old people's centre in a new housing scheme. This use has enabled the open hall to be restored, indicating the original proportions of the building.

This redundant chapel at Lavenham has been converted to a house. The inserted dormers are rather out of character, and break the roof lines.

building is not considered to be of any particular architectural merit, and the decision to convert it taken mainly on economic grounds, the alterations may well be of quite a drastic nature. The final result can be an interesting, even attractive building, but it will not necessarily bear much resemblance to the original design. If, though, the conversion is being carried out primarily for 'conservation' reasons, then it will be important to see that the character of the building and its original features are preserved intact as far as possible, and this may mean accepting a less conventional layout. In some cases, even when permission for conversion has been granted specifically to preserve a good building, the dividing line between conversion and reconstruction has proved to be very thin, and little of the original building survives intact. One feels in such cases that its existence has simply been used to obtain permission for, in effect, a new building on a site where development would not otherwise have been allowed.

A final word of warning is necessary. We often find schemes for conversion put forward, perhaps by an amenity society, simply to find a use for, and thus save, a threatened building, rather than to supply a need or demand. It is true that some good buildings have been saved by this approach, but it is most important to be as sure as possible that the proposed new use will be, and will remain, economically viable. There have been successful conversions of redundant churches into heritage centres, and old mills or factories into industrial museums, but there is clearly a limited demand for such buildings in any one area. If the new use cannot be sustained the building may revert to another period of neglect. As we shall see in a later chapter, financial aid may be available towards the cost of conversion, but in the long term the new use will probably have to be self-financing.

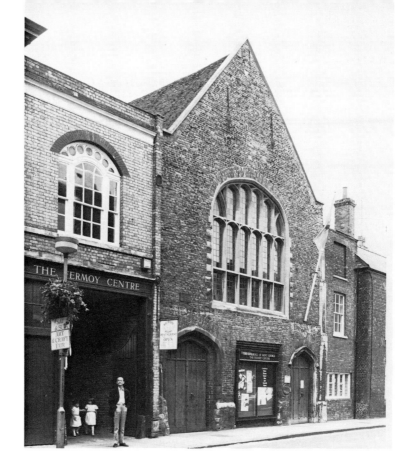

RIGHT *The medieval St George's Guildhall, King's Lynn, now a theatre and concert hall. The building was saved by a local society, and is now owned by the National Trust.*

BELOW *The former vicarage at Loughborough, largely Victorian, incorporated the remains of a medieval hall-house. When most of the house was demolished the medieval work was saved, and the original service range converted to a museum.*

3 Statutory requirements

While it is often easier to obtain planning permission for a conversion scheme than it is for a new building, there are still a number of problems which can arise, and these should be investigated before any decision is taken to acquire a building for conversion.

The first point, which is not always appreciated, is that planning permission will almost always be needed for the change of use of a building, even if no structural alterations are proposed. The only exception to this rule is when the new use is sufficiently like the existing one to come into the same Use Class under the Town and Country Planning Acts. Planning applications are normally handled by the district council. The county council may have to be consulted in certain cases, particularly if a new or altered access is required to the highway, or if the new use conflicts with an approved planning policy for the area. When determining an application the council has to take several matters into consideration. First, it must assess the appropriateness of the new use in the area, and any possible undesirable consequences such as noise or increased traffic causing danger or obstruction on the highway. In many areas there is an approved local plan, defining certain Use Zones, and it may be difficult to obtain permission for a use which does not comply with these. The effect of the alterations on the building, and on its setting, will also be considered.

If the building is in a Conservation Area, or an Area of Outstanding Natural Beauty, planning conditions may well be more stringent. The application will probably be advertised, and represen-

The old Post Office at Lichfield is now an Arts Centre. This conversion involved building an extension on the left of the original building.

RIGHT *An interesting group of maltings at Chelmsford, Essex, was once threatened by a road scheme. It has, however, been saved and converted to a shopping precinct.*

22

tations from local residents and other interested parties taken into consideration. In Conservation Areas any significant applications have to be notified to the Historic Buildings and Monuments Commission for England (see Appendix III), and its comments also considered before the application is determined.

Conditions may be even more strict if the building is listed; that is, included in the Lists of Buildings of Special Architectural or Historic Interest prepared by the Department of the Environment. The original lists were prepared in the 1950s, following the passing of the *Town and Country Planning Act* of 1947. A complete revision of the lists is due for completion in 1987, and this is resulting in a great increase in the number of listed buildings. In particular, more of the simpler, vernacular buildings and more nineteenth and early twentieth-century buildings are being included. This means that many buildings becoming available for conversion are likely to be listed, if they are of any interest or merit. The present criteria for listing, as set out below, prepared by the Department of the Environment, should make this clear:

> All buildings built before 1700 which survive in anything like their original condition are listed. Most buildings of 1700 to 1840 are listed, though selection is necessary. Between 1840 and 1914 buildings must be of definite quality and character to qualify, except where they form part of a group, and the selection is designed to include among other buildings the principal works of the principal architects.

Statutory requirements

A start is now being made on listing a very few selected buildings of 1914 to 1939. In choosing buildings, particular attention is paid to: special value within certain types, either for architectural or planning reasons, or as illustrating social and economic history (for instance, industrial buildings, railway stations, schools, hospitals, theatres, town halls, markets, exchanges, almshouses, prisons, lock-ups, mills); technological innovations or virtuosity (for instance, cast iron, prefabrication, or the early use of concrete); association with well known characters or events; group value, especially as examples of town planning (for instance, squares, terraces or model villages).

(Reproduced by kind permission of H.M. Stationery Office)

With a listed building, any alterations, *external or internal*, and including any partial demolition, will need listed building consent, in addition to any planning permission required. Clear drawings will have to be submitted to the district council, illustrating the proposals. The application is advertised, any representations received being taken into account before the council determine the application. Certain listed building applications, those affecting the more important, the Grade I and Grade II* buildings, and those in certain specified Conservation Areas, have to be notified to the Historic Buildings and Monuments Commission for England (or the equivalent bodies in Scotland, Wales and Northern Ireland), and its comments also taken into consideration. Applications involving total or partial demolition of *any* listed building have in addition to be notified to certain national amenity societies, and their comments also taken into account. In the case of Grade II listed buildings (the great majority), the district council may, after due consideration, determine the application itself, *unless* it involves total or substantial partial demolition, in which case it has to be forwarded to the Secretary of State for the Environment. *All* applications, whether they involve demolition or not, affecting Grade I or II* buildings, also have to be forwarded to the Secretary of State, with copies of all representations received. Normally the Secretary of State is required to give a decision within twenty-eight days, but this period may be extended if he requires further information or more time to consider the scheme. If he is satisfied with the proposals, he will inform the council that it may issue the decision. If, though, he is not satisfied, and in particular when there have been strong objections, he may call in the application for a public inquiry.

All these additional consultations may mean that it takes longer to obtain permission for the conversion of a listed building. On the other hand, as we have seen, it may sometimes be easier to obtain permission in such cases, particularly if the proposed use does not comply strictly with the local planning policy, but is considered to be the only means of saving a good building. When this is the case, the council will probably be particularly careful to see that the

*The old Michelin building, Fulham
Road, London. A twentieth-century
listed building, dating from 1911, it was
bought in 1985 and restored by Sir
Terence Conran and Paul Hamlyn.
Although designed before the First World
War, the building shows evidence of the
Art Deco style.*

conversion does not destroy those features which made the building worth preserving in the first place.

If planning or listed building consent is refused by the council, or if unacceptable conditions are imposed, the applicant has the right to appeal against the decision. Most planning appeals are dealt with by both parties submitting written representations, after which the site is inspected by an inspector from the Department of the Environment. In difficult or controversial cases, and more often with listed buildings or buildings in Conservation Areas, the Secretary of State may order a public inquiry at which both parties, and anyone who has submitted representations, may give evidence.

It will thus be seen that it can take a considerable time to obtain planning permission for a conversion scheme, and that the grounds for refusal may not be immediately apparent to the layman. For this reason it is always advisable to discuss the proposals with the local planning officer before taking any decision to purchase a building, whether or not the estate agent's particulars state that it is 'suitable for conversion'. Several county and district councils have published guidelines for the conversion of old buildings, and if a scheme has been prepared in accordance with this advice it is more likely to be approved without too many problems.

As well as planning permission and listed building consent,

This pair of barns at Tolpuddle, Dorset, was threatened with demolition in c. 1970. One was bought and repaired by the county council, and subsequently sold for residential conversion. Following service of a Repairs Notice, the other barn was sold, and converted by a new owner. Care was taken to insert most new windows and doors on the south frontage (RIGHT), *leaving the north (road) frontage largely unaltered.*

26

approval will probably also be necessary under the Building
Regulations. These are primarily concerned with structural safety,
matters affecting the health of the occupants, energy conservation
and means of escape in case of fire. Generally, the regulations apply
only to new, not existing, buildings, but when a building is adapted
for a new use it will have to comply with the regulations *as they
apply to that use*. This can create a number of problems. For instance,
if a domestic building is converted for a public or commercial use
the upper floors may have to be strengthened to take an increased
loading. Safety provisions in case of fire are also likely to be stricter
in such conversions, as they are when a single house is to be divided
into flats. All this work as well as involving additional expense, may
have a detrimental effect on the historic and architectural character
of the building. In the case of a listed building, a relaxation of the
regulations may be obtained in appropriate cases, but this takes
time, since applications for relaxations have to be advertised, and if
the council is not prepared to grant the relaxation the only course
open to the applicant is to appeal to the Secretary of State for the

A former chapel at Chelmsford, Essex, now houses part of the county council Institute of Higher Education.

Environment. He will have to be satisfied that a relaxation is reasonable, and will not result in danger to the building, its occupants or the public. Fortunately, some of the latest amendments to the Building Regulations are likely to simplify the conversion of old buildings. The relaxation of the requirements for minimum ceiling heights and window head heights in habitable rooms, and for space outside windows, may help to avoid the need for drastic and architecturally damaging alterations.

It will, therefore, be desirable to have an early discussion with the council's building control officer, possibly jointly with the planning officer, before any firm proposals are prepared.

Quite apart from the need to obtain approval under the Building Regulations, it must be appreciated that converting a building for a new use can often involve structural problems. An old building may have reached a state of equilibrium, any early settlement or other movement having stabilised, despite the lack of the type of foundation required today. Provided that it is left alone it will probably last for centuries, but once alterations are carried out, disturbing the subsoil, removing cross-walls, chimney stacks and floor beams, and forming new or enlarged openings, new movements may be set up, necessitating still further remedial work and in extreme cases leading to structural collapse. Even alterations to drainage, affecting the ground water level, can cause structural movement in certain cases. For this reason, unless the alterations proposed are of the simplest type, a conversion scheme should not be carried out without skilled professional advice. There are architects and surveyors who have specialised in this work and are aware of the problems. The local planning officer may be able to recommend suitable advisors, as may the Society for the Protection of Ancient Buildings (for address, see Appendix III). A structural survey should be carried out, and where serious problems are likely

LEFT and ABOVE St Anne's Gate, one of the gatehouses leading to the Close at Salisbury Cathedral, now houses an architect's office (RIGHT).

to arise, or there is any doubt about the condition of the building, the architect or surveyor may recommend employing a consultant structural engineer with experience in this type of work. The additional fees incurred will probably be more than offset by the avoidance of costly difficulties arising after the work has started. While one would not want to discourage initiative, a conversion scheme involving structural alterations to an old building is not suitable for the DIY enthusiast.

If the building is of any real architectural or historic interest, the choice of professional advisor is even more important. The architect should have a thorough knowledge of historic buildings, including the local vernacular tradition. Before any alterations are planned he should prepare an historical, as well as a structural survey, to discover the history of the building and its development, including any earlier alterations. If this is not done it is all too easy for features of interest to be destroyed. Wholesale gutting of interiors can rob a building of much of its interest, as well as creating structural problems.

The choice of the right builder for a conversion scheme is equally important. He will need to have not only the technical skills, but a real interest in this type of work, an appreciation of the need to repair and retain, rather than to renew, wherever possible, and to protect the building from damage during the work. He must also be able to be trusted to stop work and inform the architect if unforeseen problems arise, or if any unusual features are uncovered while the work is in progress. If this interest is lacking, the scheme is unlikely to be successful.

I hope that by now it will be clear that one should not expect to rush into a conversion scheme; a good deal of preliminary work is necessary, and time spent on this will probably be saved by avoiding problems and delays when the work is eventually put in hand.

4 Financial aid

Since the conversion of an old building may be quite expensive, particularly when a real effort is being made to preserve its character, it is important to be aware of the various possible sources of financial aid. First, it should be remembered that in the case of a listed building it may be possible to obtain VAT zero-rating on any work which requires, and has been granted, listed building consent. Unfortunately, this concession only applies to *alterations*, and not to repairs, a situation which sometimes encourages owners to carry out more drastic alterations than are strictly necessary, to the detriment of the historic character of the building. Despite representations by many amenity societies and environmental groups, including the Historic Buildings and Monuments Commission for England, the Treasury has so far refused to consider amending the law on this matter. Even so, this partial exemption from VAT may make the conversion of an historic building more viable. The application for exemption has to be made by the builder, and H.M. Customs and Excise have produced a leaflet giving guidance on the work normally eligible (VAT leaflet 708/85).

Coming to the question of grants, as distinct from tax allowances, these may be available from a number of sources. As will be seen, some are for *repairs* only, while others may be available for *alterations*. It will therefore be necessary in most cases to obtain separate costs for these items.

The first group of sources of aid listed below are those concerned with the preservation of historic buildings, and they are normally only available for repairs. Since, however, many old buildings being considered for conversion will also need repair, aid from these sources may be quite valuable.

Central government sources

Central government aid for most types of historic buildings is administered by the Department of the Environment, on the advice of the Historic Buildings and Monuments Commission for England, and the corresponding organisations for Wales, Scotland and Northern Ireland (for addresses, see Appendix III). These bodies consist of specialists in historic buildings, appointed by the government to advise not only on financial aid, but on listing and

Thoresby College, King's Lynn, a sixteenth-century chantry college, passed through several changes of use before being converted to old people's flats by a local Preservation Trust, with grants from central and local government and certain charitable trusts.

applications to demolish or alter historic buildings, and were set up under the *Historic Buildings and Monuments Act*, 1953, and the *National Heritage Act*, 1983. Assistance under these acts is normally only available for buildings considered to be of national importance, and in practice is generally restricted to Grade I and Grade II* buildings. Occasionally, assistance may be offered in respect of a Grade II building, particularly if its true significance was not appreciated at the time of its listing. If a Grade II building is grant-aided under this Act, it is generally up-graded to II*, thus, as we have seen, giving the Secretary of State for the Environment greater control over any future alterations.

An application for assistance under this Act has to be made by the building owner, directly to the appropriate body, and should be accompanied by as much information about the building as possible, preferably with photographs. If the authority is prepared to consider assistance, an inspector is sent to see the building and assess its importance. If he considers it to be of a sufficiently high standard to qualify for aid, the authority will send an architect to meet the building owner and his architect or other professional advisor, to agree on the necessary work and the estimated cost. Any grant offered will be based on a percentage of the cost of the eligible work. Generally, only structural repairs to the fabric are eligible, not alterations, partial demolition or normal maintenance items such as decorations, unless these become necessary as a result of the major repairs. However, although the alterations involved in conversion work will not be eligible for grant, they will have to be approved by the authority, as will the proposed new use, as being appropriate for the building.

It is important that no work is put in hand until the specification has been approved and a grant offered, as this would lead to an automatic loss of the grant. If a grant is offered, the official architect will make periodic inspections of the work to make sure that it is being carried out as approved, and in a manner appropriate to the building. No changes should be made to the approved specification without his consent, or the grant may be withdrawn. The grant is paid in instalments as the work proceeds, generally on architects' certificates.

It is often a condition of the grant that there should be some provision for public access to the building. It may have to be open to the public for a certain number of days in the year, or, if the building is of rather specialist interest, by written arrangement with the owner. If the building has few interior features of interest, access may only be required to the exterior. All classes of buildings may be eligible for assistance under the 1953 Act, but the financial means of the owner may be taken into consideration, which could affect the aid offered, for instance, in respect of commercial buildings.

It will be apparent that the numbers of buildings eligible for aid under this Act are relatively small, in relation to the total number of listed buildings. There are, however, two ways in which central government aid may be available for Grade II and even, in some cases, for unlisted buildings.

The first of these is what have come to be known as 'Section 10 Grants', i.e. grants offered under Section 10 of the *Town and Country Planning (Amendment) Act*, 1972, amended under the *Local Government and Planning Act*, 1980. This provides for assistance to be offered for work which makes a significant contribution to the character of a Conservation Area, and can include repairs to buildings. In some circumstances alterations may be assisted under this Act, particularly those which will restore or improve the character of the building (e.g. replacement of unsuitable changes in roofing materials, windows, doors, etc., by those appropriate to the building). Priority is given to work involving groups of buildings, such as a terrace, rather than to individual isolated buildings. It is obviously easier to organise a scheme of this kind if all the buildings concerned are in one ownership. Assistance may sometimes be offered in respect of a single building if the necessary works are

Financial aid

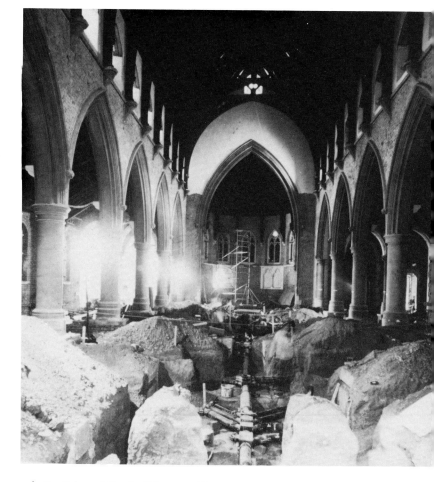

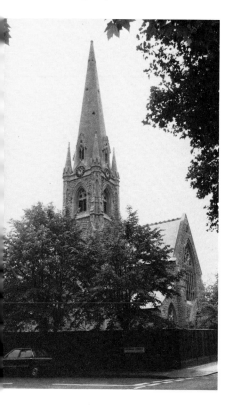

St James' Church, Myatts Park, London, during its conversion to maisonettes (for full description see pp. 226-9). The scheme was largely financed by the Housing Corporation.

substantial, and the building itself a prominent single feature of the Conservation Area. As with grants under the 1953 Act, the Commission or other body will send its own inspector and architect to assess the buildings and approve the work, including any non grant-aided items. Public access is not a condition of Section 10 grants.

The second way in which central government funds may be available for Grade II and, possibly, unlisted buildings is by means of a town scheme. These are being set up in many historic towns, and in them central and local government aid are combined.

The initiative in setting up a town scheme may come either from the county or the district council, but normally both councils will be equal partners in the eventual scheme. Having agreed to promote a town scheme the councils will approach the Department of the Environment, who will send an inspector to visit the town and discuss the scheme with the officers of the councils. A town scheme is generally based on a Conservation Area, and the inspector must be satisfied that the area, and the buildings in it, are of a sufficiently high standard to qualify. When the area to be included has been agreed, a schedule is made of all those buildings in it which would qualify for assistance. These are generally the listed buildings, but some unlisted buildings of group value may be included, and they are all marked on a map.

The councils then decide on their annual contributions to the scheme, and the Department of the Environment will match the combined figure. For instance, if the county and district councils each allocate £5,000 per annum, the Department will give £10,000, making a total annual figure of £20,000. This sum is available for grants to the approved buildings in the scheme. In most cases, a leaflet explaining the scheme and showing the buildings on a map, is prepared by the councils and distributed to the building owners. As with the grants under the 1953 Act, assistance is only available for repairs, not for alterations or normal maintenance work, but in the case of a conversion scheme any alterations will have to be approved by the Department of the Environment if a grant has been offered towards the cost of repairs.

Once the scheme is in operation, individual applications are submitted to the councils, and forwarded to the Department of the Environment for approval of the proposed works, and costs. Normally, each council will contribute ten per cent of the cost of the eligible work, and the Department of the Environment 20 per cent, making a total of 40 per cent to the owner. It will thus be seen that for a comparatively modest expenditure from each council, quite substantial help can be given to owners, and anyone planning a conversion would be well advised to find out whether a town scheme is in operation in the area.

As with Section 10 grants, public access is not normally a condition of town scheme aid. The Department of the Environment does, however, make certain other conditions. For instance, assistance is not normally offered to large-scale commercial concerns, such as multiple stores or banks, even if their buildings would qualify on architectural grounds. It is, therefore, important for the councils to consult the Department of the Environment on each application before offering or promising assistance.

The National Heritage Memorial Fund (for address, see Appendix III) is another possible source of central government grant aid, but probably only in exceptional cases. This fund was set up to assist by grant or loan the acquisition, maintenance or preservation of buildings and other works of art of outstanding importance. It is not likely that many buildings being considered for conversion will fall into this category, but in the case of, say, a surviving building of a very rare type it may be worth investigating this source.

Application may be made for aid from more than one central government source, but it should be noted that the total amount of grant from these is rarely more than 50 per cent of the cost of eligible work. Central government aid is not normally offered in respect of newly purchased property, but this rule is sometimes relaxed when the building has been purchased specifically to preserve it, when it might otherwise have been lost. With all central government aid also, any grant will normally have to be paid back if the building is sold within a specified period after receipt of grant.

Local government sources

Under the *Local Authorities (Historic Buildings) Act, 1962,* any local authority, county or district council may offer grants and/or loans for the repair of historic buildings. Unlisted buildings may be eligible if the council considers them to be of sufficient historic interest, for instance in a Conservation Area where unlisted buildings may be of group value. These grants and loans are entirely at the councils' discretion. Some councils do not offer them at all, and those that do so vary considerably in the amounts available and the conditions attached. Loans may be at any rate of interest, or be interest free, and the councils may decide on any period of repayment.

This assistance can often be helpful in 'topping up' Section 10 or town scheme grants. If the owner is having difficulty in finding his share of the cost, the council may offer a grant or loan for all or part of the balance. As with central government grants, most councils will not offer assistance if work is started before approval has been given, and the standard of work will have to be appropriate to the building. Grants and loans under this Act are not available for alteration or conversion work, but help with repairs may make a conversion scheme more viable. Any grant, or the balance of any loan, will probably have to be repaid if the building is sold within a specified period after it has been paid.

Private and voluntary sources

There are a number of private and voluntary trusts and funds which may make grants for the repair of historic buildings. Some of these operate nationally and will assist a wide range of buildings, while others are restricted to helping certain classes of building; others again operate in particular areas. One very useful source of information about such funds is the *Directory of Grant-Making Trusts,* published annually by CAF Publications Ltd of Tonbridge, Kent. As well as listing the trusts under headings indicating the causes they help, it gives useful advice on making an application. Some of these trusts may assist work of conversion, as well as repairs, and in many cases it will be easier to obtain help from such trusts for buildings which are to be used for some community purpose, rather than as private houses or business premises. Some of the national amenity societies, such as the Society for the Protection of Ancient Buildings (for address, see Appendix III), may be able to advise on other voluntary sources of aid.

Apart from these sources, which are concerned mainly with the *preservation* of historic buildings, there are others which may help in putting redundant buildings to new and viable uses, with less emphasis on their historic and architectural importance. Grants from these sources may be available both for repairs and for alterations.

Department of the Environment

Quite apart from the historic buildings grants described above, several forms of aid may be obtained from the Department for conversion works, but some of these are restricted to certain parts of Great Britain, or to particular users.

Under the urban programme, assistance may be offered to local authorities in England for work which can help in the regeneration of certain inner city areas with problems of economic decline and physical decay. This can include conversion of buildings for housing, industrial, commercial and educational uses, and the grant may be up to 75 per cent of the local authority expenditure. Application should be made to the Department of the Environment (for address, see Appendix III). Under the Urban Development Grant Scheme, similar assistance may be available for private companies working with the local authority. Priority is given to enterprise zones and other designated districts. Most of these are in inner city areas, but a few wider areas have been included. Eligible work can include the conversion of redundant buildings to provide housing, employment and other social facilities. The amount of grant varies, but it is expected that the private companies will invest three or four times the amount of the grant. Application should be made to the local office of the Department of the Environment.

The Department, in conjunction with the Royal Institute of British Architects, also administers the Community Projects Fund. This can provide grants towards the cost of preparing a feasibility study, by an architect or other professional advisor, into the viability of a scheme of restoration or conversion. The project must be one of benefit to the community. This can be a help to a voluntary organisation wondering whether it will be worthwhile embarking on a particular project. Application should be made to the Community Architecture Office, Royal Institute of British Architects (for address, see Appendix III). Somewhat similar assistance may be available from the Department of the Environment under the Urban Initiatives Grants Scheme, which concentrates on inner city areas. This is administered by the Civic Trust (for address, see Appendix III), to whom application should be made.

The Development Commission

This Commission, a central government body, may make grants of up to 25 per cent of the costs towards converting redundant

A redundant barn at Odstock, near Salisbury, converted to a
silk-screen printing works, with assistance from CoSIRA.

buildings in certain priority areas in England, for light industrial, including craft, use. The priority areas are those where there is considered to be a shortage of rural employment opportunity, and the main areas currently (1987) are the Southwest, parts of East Anglia, the Welsh Border, and the North and Northeast. These grants are administered by the Council for Small Industries in Rural Areas (CoSIRA). The Council's head office is in Salisbury (for address, see Appendix III), but there are local offices in many parts of England, where the first approach should be made. As with some historic buildings grants, these grants are repayable if the building is sold soon after completion of the work. In addition to administering these grants, CoSIRA can help in other ways. It may make loans towards the cost of conversion, and put owners of redundant buildings in touch with potential users.

Similar schemes are in operation in Scotland and Wales, administered by the Scottish and Welsh Development Agencies, and Mid-Wales Development (for addresses, see Appendix III). The Development Commission may also make grants to convert buildings into village halls in rural development areas. These are administered directly by the Commission (for address, see Appendix III).

Tourist boards

The English, Scottish and Welsh tourist boards may offer assistance towards the conversion of buildings for purposes connected with the promotion of tourism. This can include such things as hotel, hostel or self-catering accommodation, leisure facilities and similar attractions. Most of this assistance is in the form of grants, but it can

RIGHT *Part of a group of farm buildings at Osmington, Dorset, converted to holiday cottages with assistance from the English Tourist Board.*

*Another view of the Osmington scheme.
The buildings are grouped round the
original farmyard. The windows are
perhaps rather over-domestic in
character.*

include loans. Grants are normally between 15 and 20 per cent of the cost, and are only offered when the work could not be carried out without this assistance.

As with other sources of aid, various conditions are attached, and it is important not to start work until the scheme has been approved. Application should be made to the appropriate tourist board (for address, see Appendix III). The tourist boards can also advise on the viability of particular schemes, and on the relevant legislation.

Department of Trade and Industry

Under the Regional Development Grants Scheme, the Department of Trade and Industry may provide grants for work which will create employment, including the conversion of buildings for industrial use. These are available in regional development areas, mainly in the Northeast and the Northwest. Application should be made to the Department of Trade and Industry (for address, see Appendix III).

A group of farm buildings at Tincleton, Dorset, partly converted and partly rebuilt as holiday cottages, with assistance from the English Tourist Board.

The Countryside Commission (England and Wales) and the Countryside Commission for Scotland

These Commissions, also central government bodies, may give grants for the creation of countryside interpretation centres. Such centres may be run by local authorities, private organisations such as museums, or by individuals. While many of these are based in new purpose-built structures, suitable existing buildings may be used, particularly if they are of local historic interest. The siting of the building, as well as its design, will clearly be of vital importance in deciding on the viability of such a use. The Commissions will advise on the suitability of buildings and on the setting up of the centre. Application should be made to the appropriate Commission (for addresses, see Appendix III).

The Manpower Services Commission (renamed The Training Commission)

When a building is to be converted for some public or community use, assistance can sometimes be obtained through the Commission, provided that the scheme complies with the Commission's criteria for the community programme, and that funds are available. This programme is designed to provide temporary employment, usually for one year, for unemployed people. If the scheme is approved by the Commission it will cover the wages of the people employed, leaving the building owner, or sponsor, to provide the materials.

Some very worthwhile schemes have been carried out in this way, but the possible problems should not be underestimated. It is essential to have a skilled and responsible supervisor. Many community programme schemes are sponsored by local authorities, and anyone wondering whether to carry out a conversion scheme in this way would be well advised to contact the county or district council to see whether they can offer any help or advice.

The headquarters of the Commission is in Sheffield (for address, see Appendix III), but schemes are administered from local offices over the country.

The Housing Corporation

The Housing Corporation (for address, see Appendix III) is responsible for the funding, supervision and registration of housing associations. Up to 80 per cent grant may be available for the provision of housing to rent, and this can include the conversion of buildings for this purpose. The work has to be approved by the Corporation as creating housing units of an acceptable standard.

Assistance is only offered to registered housing associations, not to private landlords or commercial concerns.

The Sports Council

The Sports Council (for address, see Appendix III) may give grants and/or interest-free loans for the creation of sports facilities, and this can include the purchase and conversion of buildings for this purpose. Before offering a grant, the Council must be assured that a management arrangement can be secured, and that an adequate proportion of the local community can use the facilities. The maximum grant is normally 50 per cent, but this can be supplemented by a loan, up to a combined total of 75 per cent if it would not otherwise be possible to carry out the scheme. Private individuals, voluntary organisations, companies and local authorities may all be eligible for assistance.

The organisation applying for assistance must either be the freehold owner of the building concerned, or entitled to a lease of at least twenty-eight years, to obtain the maximum grant. Buildings held on shorter leases will attract a lower proportion of grant. If the building is subsequently sold, or if the conditions imposed by the Sports Council are not complied with, the grant and/or loan may have to be repaid. The Council must be satisfied about the viability of the scheme, and the ability of the applicant organisation to raise the rest of the capital cost, and be responsible for the subsequent running costs. Certain other conditions may be imposed, and the scheme must be approved and an offer of assistance made before any work is started or, if assistance is being sought towards the cost of purchasing a building, before any contract of sale is signed. At present (1987) the minimum grant is £750, the minimum cost of the project being £1,500. For loans the figures are £1,000 and £2,000 respectively. Applications should be made to the appropriate regional office of the Sports Council.

Local authorities

Apart from assistance under the *Historic Buildings Act*, local authorities may be able to help conversion schemes in other ways. Some county and district councils give grants and/or loans towards the cost of providing village halls, old people's day centres, and other community buildings. It is always worthwhile asking whether such aid is available for conversion schemes for such purposes.

District, but not county, councils may also give assistance under the Housing Acts. Conversion of a large house into flats, or the conversion of a non-residential building for residential use may be eligible for improvement grants. These are made at the discretion of the local authority, and councils have differing policies about their use for this purpose, as distinct from the improvement of existing sub-standard houses. The amount of grant is fixed by the government each year, and part of it may be used for repairs necessitated by the conversion. Higher grant limits are generally available for listed buildings.

If a grant is offered under the Housing Acts, the council will have to approve the specification, and be satisfied that the resultant house or houses come up to its standards. It may in fact require additional work to be carried out, and there can sometimes be problems if compliance with the council's standards conflicts with the maintenance of the historic character of the building. Councils have power to relax their standard requirements in the case of listed buildings. For this reason, and because any possible grant will be forfeited if the work starts before the scheme has been approved, an early discussion with the appropriate council officer is essential.

The European Economic Community

It may be possible to obtain grants from the European Economic Community, for conversion schemes which are designed to promote tourism. These grants are generally administered through the national tourist boards, who should be able to advise on the likelihood of any such aid, and the preparation of the necessary applications.

Assistance, generally of rather a limited nature, may also be available from the Community for restoring historic buildings for cultural and educational activities. Application should be made to the address in Appendix III.

Building preservation trusts

Some very successful conversion schemes have been carried out by building preservation trusts, some of them having been set up specifically to save a threatened building. The main purpose of these trusts is to acquire and repair historic buildings in danger of demolition or neglect. They may be sponsored by a local authority, or be independent organisations. They are generally based on a particular area, such as a county, a district or a town.

Trusts may deal with their buildings, after repair, in two ways. Some trusts prefer to retain the buildings, letting them to suitable tenants, using the rent income for maintenance, and to help finance further work. Others prefer to recover their capital by selling the buildings, subject to covenants. Where the main purpose of a trust is to provide housing, it may be registered as a housing association under the Industrial and Provident Societies Acts, thus, as we have seen, enabling it to obtain substantial assistance from the Housing Corporation. Other forms of constitution may be more appropriate where the provision of housing is not the main aim of the trust, and legal and financial advice should be obtained. The Civic Trust (for address, see Appendix III), which maintains a register of approved preservation trusts, will be able to give advice, and has prepared a model constitution.

All trusts may apply for assistance to the Historic Buildings and Monuments Commission for England, and the equivalent Welsh, Scottish and Northern Ireland organisations, to the local authorities, to private and charitable trusts, and, depending on the location and proposed use of the building concerned, to the other bodies described in this chapter. One very useful source of help is the Architectural Heritage Fund, administered by the Civic Trust. This fund can offer low-interest loans to approved trusts to enable them to buy and repair property, the loan being repaid either out of the proceeds of sale after completion of the repairs, or from rent income if the property is retained by the trust. Trusts may also accept individual subscriptions and donations, and may launch public appeals for funds.

In view of the variety of sources of possible financial aid, their application to particular schemes, and the conditions attached (which may vary from time to time), as well as the taxation implications—in particular when buildings are being converted for subsequent resale—it is important to obtain professional financial and legal advice before embarking on a conversion scheme of any size.

The Old House at Home, Dorchester, Dorset, a former inn, threatened with demolition and bought by the district council following service of a Repairs Notice. It was then bought and repaired (RIGHT) *as a private house by a Preservation Trust.*

Hyde Barn, Winchester, converted to a historic resources centre (for full description see p. 90).

Part II. Building types

5 Farm buildings

Old farm buildings often become available for conversion, due to changes in farming practice, which may make them less suited to their original uses. In some cases, of course, they are demolished and replaced by new buildings, and when this does not happen it is probably for one of two reasons. On the one hand they may be listed buildings, and permission for demolition refused, but on the other hand more farmers and landowners are now realising the commercial potential either of converting the buildings themselves, or of selling them with planning permission for conversion. This is particularly common when farms are amalgamated, making groups or single buildings redundant, in positions where the landowner would not necessarily object to a new occupant.

Barns

Farm buildings are of many types, including some found only in particular areas, but the ones probably most often considered for conversion are the large barns, originally built for grain or fodder storage, often combined with threshing. The barn may be part of a group of buildings, including the farmhouse, grouped round a yard; it may stand in a village street, a relic of pre-enclosure farming, or it may be an isolated field barn, perhaps incorporating a stockman's cottage. Clearly the siting of a barn will affect its potential for conversion.

Large barns of this type may be of medieval date—one thinks in particular of the large stone barns built by the religious houses to store the produce of their estates, often buildings of some architectural pretensions. Barns continued to be built throughout the sixteenth and seventeenth centuries, but the majority of those surviving today are probably of eighteenth or nineteenth century date. We find them built in a variety of materials: stone, flint, cob and brick, or timber framed and weatherboarded. On the older barns the roofs were generally thatched, although stone slates might have been used on the large monastic or manorial barns. Later, tiles and slates were used, often replacing thatch, while in recent times the original covering has often been replaced with corrugated iron or asbestos. Aisled barns are sometimes found, particularly in eastern England, and many barns, even as late as the eighteenth century,

Former stables at Avebury, Wiltshire, now a museum.

had interesting roof structures, designed to cover a wide span with the minimum of internal obstruction. A common feature of most types of barn is the through-way, formed by pairs of opposed doors, designed to admit waggons, and to allow a through draught to facilitate hand-threshing.

While considering different types of barn, we should include the long-house and the laithe-house, where the barn (or byre) is attached to the farmhouse. In the long-house, typical of the north and west, as far south as Dartmoor, the house and byre are generally of approximately equal length, and are connected internally. In the laithe-house, typical of parts of Yorkshire, the house is generally smaller than the barn, and there is no internal communication between them.

Although simple and functional in design, old barns are often very attractive, and this is no doubt why they are such popular subjects for conversion. It is, though, all too easy to destroy in the process of conversion those very features which give the barn its character; the large unbroken roof slopes, and the open interior with its interesting roof structure. The best conversion schemes, and the most suitable new uses, are those which retain these characteristics as far as possible.

Where a barn forms part of a farm group, and the other buildings, including perhaps the house, are to remain in agricultural use, the possibilities for conversion are clearly limited. Sometimes such barns, no longer wanted for their original use, have been altered for other agricultural purposes. This may be the best solution, but it can result in rather unsympathetic alterations and additions. Other suitable uses in these circumstances are farm shops, a craft or light industry which is compatible with farming, or simply storage, either for the farm or rented out. In all these cases the planning authority will need to be satisfied that any extra traffic generated will not be a safety hazard, and, in the case of craft or light industry, that this will not cause future problems by outgrowing its original conception.

Where the barn does not form part of a continuing farm complex, the possibilities for conversion are generally greater. Let us look

A timber-framed and brick-nogged barn at Holly Tree Farm, Hoton near Loughborough, used as a craft workshop. The rear entrance doors have been replaced by glazing (BELOW), the only external alteration.

next at the barn which stands in a village street, rather than in a farmyard. A surprisingly large number of these have survived, in spite of the effect of the parliamentary enclosures. Barns in these situations have been converted for a number of purposes which enable their essential character to be retained. Village or community halls, theatres, museums and exhibition halls, shops, craft workshops, restaurants and sports halls can all, if carefully designed, maintain the open interior and unbroken roof lines of the original building.

Often, though, the most profitable scheme proves to be a residential conversion. Very high prices are paid for barns with planning permission for this, but all too often it results in a drastic change of character, particularly if, in order to make the maximum profit, a barn is divided into two or more units. Additional doors and windows of 'domestic' character are inserted, and the roof is broken by a series of dormers and brick chimneys. Internally, intermediate floors are inserted, and if the original roof trusses cause obstruction in the upper storey they may be altered or removed.

Such a 'conversion' can be almost, if not quite, as damaging as complete demolition and rebuilding, and, indeed, it often amounts to just that.

With the isolated field barns, the conversion possibilities may be rather different. Use for craft or light industry may be acceptable to the planning authority, but any form of 'public' use is less likely to be approved, if it is thought that this will result in increased traffic on unsuitable roads. Residential conversion may be allowed, particularly if the barn is of real architectural merit, and the scheme is designed to preserve its character, but some authorities do not encourage the creation of, in effect, new residential units in the open countryside. In some areas, though, the use of redundant buildings for tourist purposes is being encouraged, and this could include conversion into holiday accommodation. This latter use has the advantage of often requiring less alteration and modernisation than a normal residential conversion. The Landmark Trust (for address, see Appendix III) has carried out some excellent schemes of this type.

Another use which has been found for some of these isolated barns is as shelters and overnight camping barns for walkers and cyclists. Some have been converted for this use in the Yorkshire Dales National Park with the help of the Countryside Commission (for address, see Appendix III). See also Appendix II. These have proved popular, but, although the exteriors of the barns have been carefully preserved, the requirements of the Building, Fire and Public Health Regulations have sometimes meant that considerable internal alterations have had to be carried out, far beyond the original

Formerly a village barn with an unbroken stone wall and roof, this building now has irregular and obtrusive fenestration. When planning committees give permission for this sort of development, both the building and the environment are the poorer.

50

A converted barn in the Yorkshire Dales.

intentions of the sponsors and inevitably destroying something of the original character of the barns. In Derbyshire, in the Peak District National Park, a similar scheme has been started, and here it was possible to avoid some of the problems encountered in Yorkshire by persuading the authorities to regard the barns as 'stone tents' on camping sites. This has enabled them to be kept as simple basic shelters but, in order to avoid the Yorkshire problems, they can only be used by organisations exempted under the *Camping and Caravanning Act*. In the original pilot scheme their use was restricted to the Girl Guides, but the Peak Park Joint Planning Board has now been recognized as an exempted organisation in its own right, and the scheme is being extended.

Having considered some of the possible uses for redundant barns, we should look at some of the problems likely to be met in their conversion. The first essential step will be a thorough survey of the building, both structural and historical. As we have seen in an earlier chapter, it is important to be sure that the barn is sufficiently sound to stand the alterations involved. It is also advantageous to work out the original form of the building, and any later alterations and additions. Some later additions of an unsympathetic nature may be best removed, but the addition of, say, a wheelhouse for an early horse-drawn threshing machine may add interest to the barn, and be worth incorporating in the new scheme. If the original roof covering has been replaced with, for instance, corrugated sheeting, it will often be desirable to replace this with the original, or at least a more appropriate material.

The structural problems likely to be encountered will depend

both on the construction of the barn, and the use to which it will be put. Let us start with the timber-framed barns, generally weatherboarded externally, found in many parts of the country. These vary considerably in the standard of construction, the earlier barns generally having the most substantial timbers. For most uses it will be necessary to improve the weather-resistance and heat insulation standards of the structure, and to insert some form of damp-proof course in the wall base. In some cases, particularly where the intermediate timbers are of light construction, the best way to deal with this problem will be to build up an independent internal lining wall, which can also be used to support any inserted floors, thus avoiding any additional loading on the original walls. It may be possible to expose the main posts internally. Care will have to be taken when excavating for foundations for the new inner wall, not to undermine the original wall base.

If the main walling timbers are substantial, and it is desired to expose these internally, it may be possible to fit a suitable insulating infilling between them. Unlike timber-framed houses, most barns had no infilling, since ventilation was more important than insulation. In these cases it may be necessary to refix the external weatherboarding on building paper, to improve weather resistance, but care must be taken not to create conditions encouraging condensation within the wall.

A timber-framed barn at Barnston, Essex, showing conversion in progress (BELOW), *and after completion* (ABOVE) . *External alterations have been minimised.*

A group of barns at West Lulworth, Dorset, converted to houses. Although several dormers have been inserted, the buildings have retained something of their agricultural character.

Some form of roof insulation will also probably be necessary, and this can often be combined with the renewal of the roof covering if this has to be done. If the roof is thatched, a fire-resisting lining can often be inserted at the same time. While it will generally be desirable to expose the main roof trusses, especially if these are of an interesting design, the decision whether or not to expose the common rafters will depend on their form and condition. If they are rather thin, as is often found in later barns, and if they need a considerable amount of renewal, they may be better covered by a new ceiling.

With substantial brick and stone barns, it may not be necessary to build up an internal wall lining, but damp-proofing, including the insertion of a damp-proof course, will be necessary for most uses, and if any inserted floors are to be carried on the existing walls the local authority will have to be satisfied that they can take the additional load. In the case of cob barns, which are generally built off a brick, flint or stone base, it may be possible to insert a damp-proof course in this, but care should be taken not to dry out cob walling excessively, as this could cause shrinkage and possible failure. For this reason, the construction of an inner wall lining, or the use of a waterproof lathing to take new plaster, may be a better alternative.

Most barns have plain earth floors, and for most uses these will

have to be replaced by solid floors incorporating a damp-proof membrane. By preventing moisture evaporating through the floor, this can drive it up the walls, a factor which must be taken into consideration when deciding on the best method of damp proofing.

Although many barns consist, internally, of a single unbroken space, some do have an intermediate floor over part of the area, and perhaps some integral cross-walls. If the conversion scheme involves the removal of these floors or walls, which are probably helping to stabilise the structure, care must be taken to see that this is not weakened by the alterations. The design of most barns, a single open space without internal cross-walls, means that any failure or defect of the roof structure can cause additional thrust on the walls, which may lean outwards and ultimately collapse if no remedial action is taken. It is for this reason that we often find buttresses added to barns, but these, unless they are carefully designed and built, may be ineffective and even increase movement in the walls. It is sometimes better to secure the walls by ties at eaves level, or by inserting a reinforced concrete ring beam. The roof structure must be repaired as necessary to remove the source of the trouble. The aim should be to repair the walls in-situ if possible, rather than rebuilding them, particularly in early barns where it is difficult to reproduce the original texture. In designing the conversion, any new cross-walls can be used to help stabilise the structure.

Barns at Cattistock, Dorset, converted for residential use. They occupy a prominent position at the approach to the village.

This conversion of a fine late medieval barn (a Grade II* listed building) at Lillington, Dorset, has been very sensitively handled. Only the chimney and television aerial indicate its domestic use.

As previously stated, the best uses for barns, particularly where the interior is of high quality, are those which involve the minimum of alteration, thus enabling the size of the barn and its roof structure to remain intact and visible for most, if not all, of its length. Domestic conversion, probably the most popular and profitable, is the one most likely to cause problems in this respect. Conversion to a single house is nearly always preferable to the creation of several small units, unless the barn is of exceptional size, since it will involve the insertion of fewer new door and window openings. If a converted barn is to retain anything of its authenticity it must be accepted that the design will not be that of a conventional house. Internal divisions should be kept to a minimum, by adopting an open-plan layout, and part at least should remain open to the roof to enable the scale of the interior to be appreciated. If there is insufficient height to enable a floor to be inserted without destroying the roof trusses, a single-storey house may have to be accepted. On the other hand, the recent modifications to the Building Regulations regarding ceiling heights can be helpful. Sometimes the less important rooms, such as kitchens, bathrooms, minor bedrooms and cloakrooms, can be planned on the ground floor, with ceilings of minimum height, and the living rooms placed on the upper floor. In other cases an interesting galleried effect can be obtained. A flexible approach to the internal planning is essential.

55

A barn at Fisherton Delamere, Wiltshire, on a steeply sloping site, converted into a house. The attic partitions (TOP) have been fitted into the existing roof trusses.

Doors and windows should be formed in existing openings as far as possible, and kept simple in character, dark stained timber generally being more appropriate than painted woodwork. Pseudo 'Tudor' or 'Georgian' features should be avoided. It is often possible to insert large areas of glazing in the old cart entrances, to provide adequate lighting, and dormers should be kept to a minimum. Windows can sometimes be inserted in the end gable walls to help light the upper storey. Sometimes flush roof lights are preferable to dormers, particularly in dark coloured roofs such as slate. If there is sufficient internal headroom, inset dormers, avoiding any projection from the roof line, may be acceptable. The insertion of fireplaces can present a problem, as brick chimney stacks easily give the building too 'domestic' a character, and sometimes the use of a plain metal flue is preferable. The aim should be to retain the agricultural character of the barn as far as possible. See Appendix I.

Whatever new use is adopted, there may well be problems with the Building, Fire and Public Health Regulations, and early discussions with the appropriate officers are essential. For some public uses the owner may be asked to cover all or most of the exposed timbers with a fire-resisting cladding, to the detriment of the internal appearance, but this can sometimes be avoided by carrying out charring tests on the timbers, to check that timber of sufficient strength will survive a fire, and, possibly, by treating the timbers with a colourless fire-resisting coating. In this context, it may be necessary to apply for a relaxation of the regulations, and this is often easier to obtain if the building is listed. It must be admitted that local authorities vary considerably in the flexibility of their attitudes in these matters, as we have seen in the case of the camping barns in Yorkshire and Derbyshire.

Most barns are quite large, but if additions are necessary they should be of a traditional form. Lean-tos flanking a projecting cart porch, with the main roof carried down over them as catslides, can be quite successful. If it is necessary to lengthen the building, the roof of the extension is best kept below that of the main barn, and its walls set back slightly, so that the form of the original barn is still apparent. This is particularly important if the materials of the new extension are not an exact match for those of the original building.

However carefully the conversion may have been carried out, the treatment of its surroundings is equally important. A 'suburban' style garden to a house, or a plethora of signs and obtrusive car parking space in front of a community building or restaurant can be almost as damaging as unsympathetic alterations to the barn itself.

Before leaving the subject of barn conversion we should consider the question of moving and re-erecting barns on new sites, generally for a new use. This is becoming increasingly popular, especially with timber-framed barns. Although there is evidence that timber-framed buildings have been moved and re-erected from quite early times, there is inevitably some loss of historic character if a building is re-erected on an urban or suburban site. In some cases,

A timber-framed barn moved and re-erected as a cricket pavilion at Singleton, Sussex.

though, this may be the only alternative to the complete loss of the building, and it is more justifiable if the barn is of special intrinsic value, for instance if the roof design is of an unusual and interesting type.

If a barn is to be moved in this way, the dismantling and re-erection will have to be carried out with great care. A thorough survey should be made, with careful measured drawings and photographs, and the timbers numbered and marked on the drawing to ensure that they are replaced in their original positions. It is almost inevitable that more renewal will be needed than would have been the case had the barn been repaired in-situ, but this should be kept to a minimum if the finished result is not to look over-restored and contrived. If the barn is listed, listed building consent will of course be required both for the dismantling and the re-erection, and the latter will also need planning and Building Regulation approval. Since the new site for the barn may be in a different local authority area from its original one, prior consultations with both councils will be advisable.

Other farm buildings

Redundant farm buildings at Pamphill, Dorset, converted into a farm shop and restaurant.

Apart from the large barns, other farm buildings are sometimes available for conversion, the most common perhaps being complete farm complexes, grouped around a yard and sometimes including the farmhouse, which has become redundant as a result of the amalgamation of two or more small farms. These groups may be near a village, or on isolated sites. As well as the house and the main barn, these complexes usually include stables, cowsheds, cart sheds and granaries. The buildings may be all of one date and style, as in some late eighteenth and nineteenth-century 'model' farms, or they may be of different dates, materials and general quality.

From an architectural point of view it is nearly always best if the conversion of a farm group of this type is carried out as a unified scheme, even if the buildings are subsequently to be sold or let to different occupants. If, as so often happens, they are sold off separately once planning permission has been granted for a new use, the result may be rather an unhappy hotchpotch, with the standard of design and construction varying considerably among the buildings, and the virtual impossibility of creating a unified scheme of landscaping.

Farm complexes have been converted for a number of uses, including residential units (either for permanent or holiday use), craft workshops or light industry, possibly combined with some residential use, interpretation centres, shops, restaurants, field study centres, youth hostels and similar simple holiday accommodation. If the site is in, or on, the outskirts of a village or town, a farm complex can sometimes become a community centre, making use of the different buildings for various activities.

When considering any change of use, the planning authority will have to look at the suitability of the site, including the provision of adequate and safe access. In particular, if the buildings are approached by narrow country roads, any likely increase in traffic for the new use will probably be a major consideration. As in the case of single barns, though, some councils will encourage the use of farm groups for light industrial or for tourist purposes.

It is only natural that the owner or developer of a farm complex being considered for conversion should want to make the maximum profit from the scheme, and there is often a desire to obtain the greatest possible usable or lettable space from every building on the site, regardless of its suitability, or architectural or structural quality. Where the buildings are of varying dates, there are likely to be some (generally the later ones) of rather poor quality, whose conversion would inevitably amount to a substantial rebuilding. There may also be cases where, as a result of additions to the original group, some buildings are too close together to allow for a satisfactory plan. It may often be necessary to consider demolishing some of the later and poorer buildings in the group. This is less likely to be the case with 'model' or planned farmyards than with those where development has been more haphazard. Once the overall plan has been decided, each building will have to be assessed individually, the aim being to carry out the conversion in such a way as to make the best use, and retain the character, of each building rather than to replan them all to fit in with a stereotyped scheme, with the consequent loss of their individuality.

Let us now look at the various buildings of the farmyard, with their possibilities for conversion.

Stables

These are found in many forms. At the simplest level we have the single farm stable, perhaps with a hay loft above it. On larger farms there could be a range of such stables, with the typical two-part doors, and one or more loft doors on the upper floors, sometimes in gabled dormers. Access to the upper floor is often by a flight of external steps against a gable wall. Apart from the farm stables for working horses, we find stables for the carriage horses attached to, or in, the grounds of country or town houses. These may be combined with a coach house, and harness room, and have living quarters for a groom as well as a hay loft on the upper floor. At the highest social level there may be a stable and coach house block of

Residential conversion of a stable at Stratford-sub-Castle, Wiltshire. All new openings have been made in the inner facade, leaving the road frontage (BELOW) unaltered.

some architectural pretensions, perhaps built round a courtyard. All these become available for conversion.

Where simple farm stables are found as part of a farm complex, they may be converted for a variety of uses, but can often be adapted quite successfully for simple holiday or 'motel' type units. The stable doors should be retained, with some simple glazing in the upper leaf if required. The upper storey is likely to be an attic only, and may need additional lighting. In a single building this can often be provided by windows in the gable end walls, avoiding the need for inserted dormers, and by glazing the original loft doors. In a range of such stables, in order to provide units of more adequate size, two stables may be combined to form one cottage, but if possible the old doors and windows should be retained to preserve the rhythm of the façade. If fireplaces are required, simple metal flues may be more appropriate than a range of brick chimneys.

The stables and coach houses associated with private houses,

An interesting residential conversion of a coach house at Worcester.

rather than farms, have further possibilities for conversion. Sometimes another residential unit can be formed, subject to planning permission. If it is not possible to create a separate curtilage and access for this, any permission may be subject to a condition forbidding the sale of the new unit separately from the main house. The original coach house, with its large doors, may become the garage, and as the upper floor often comprised a flat for the groom, a residential use should present few problems. Indeed, in London and other towns, mews conversions have for long been popular. Another use for such buildings could be for craft or light industry,

A range of old stables, leading off the main street at Marlborough, Wiltshire, converted to a shopping precinct.

either associated with the house or separately let. Here again the planning authority will need to be satisfied that no nuisance will be created by the new use, but it could well be supported if it is the council's policy to create opportunities for small-scale employment in the area.

The large formal stable and coach house ranges associated with major country houses have been converted for many uses. Where the house is open to the public the stables may be used to house some subsidiary attraction, such as a museum, shop or tea room. Such buildings are now often listed in their own right, separately from the house, and any conversion scheme will have to be carefully designed to avoid spoiling their character, in particular by the insertion of unsuitable doors and windows. As we have seen with barns, for most uses stables will have to be given an adequate damp-proofing system, the method used depending on the construction of the original building.

Cart sheds

These may be single-storey buildings, or two-storeyed, with a hay loft, granary or other store above the cart shed itself, approached by an external stair on the gable wall. The cart shed is generally open at the front, the roof of a single-storey building, or the upper floor if there is one, being supported on brick or stone piers or timber posts. Sometimes the front wall of the upper storey is timber-framed and weatherboarded, to reduce the load on these posts.

In any conversion scheme it is best for the lower storey to remain open at the front if possible, and it can often be used for covered car parking or similar use. The upper storey can be used for various purposes associated with the overall scheme for the complex, but it will probably be necessary to improve the weather resistance of any timber-framed wall, and the fire resistance of the first floor. As with other farm buildings, where the upper storey is simply a loft or attic, partly in the roof space, insertion of dormers should be kept to a minimum, making use of any loft doors, and windows in the gable ends. If it is necessary to fill in the open frontage of the lower storey, this should be done in such a way as to leave evidence of the original design, perhaps by letting the piers project and by designing the infilling in timber and glass, to retain something of the original open character.

Granaries

Although, as we have seen, the upper storey of a cart shed was sometimes used as a granary (the open area below helping to provide ventilation for the stored grain), separate granaries were often built. Many of these are timber-framed, weatherboarded externally, with gabled or often hipped roofs, and raised on staddle stones, partly to allow air circulation below the floor, and partly to deter rats. Sometimes granaries are of stone or brick, with the floor raised over arches or piers.

Some of the more substantial granaries have been converted into houses, but this has often involved building quite large extensions which have partly destroyed the original scale and character of the buildings. It is generally better to find some other use, such as a workshop, small shop, store or club room. The timber-framed granaries are more difficult to convert, requiring considerable improvements to make them really weatherproof and to provide insulation of an acceptable standard for most uses. Such a building might become a simple office, information centre or store, in conjunction with an overall farm scheme.

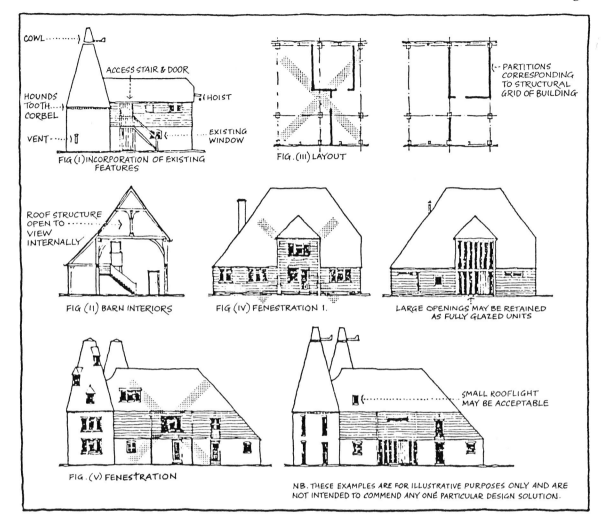

COWL

ACCESS STAIR & DOOR

HOUNDS TOOTH CORBEL

VENT

HOIST

EXISTING WINDOW

FIG (I) INCORPORATION OF EXISTING FEATURES

FIG. (III) LAYOUT

PARTITIONS CORRESPONDING TO STRUCTURAL GRID OF BUILDING

ROOF STRUCTURE OPEN TO VIEW INTERNALLY

FIG (II) BARN INTERIORS

FIG (IV) FENESTRATION 1.

LARGE OPENINGS MAY BE RETAINED AS FULLY GLAZED UNITS

SMALL ROOFLIGHT MAY BE ACCEPTABLE

FIG. (V) FENESTRATION

NB. THESE EXAMPLES ARE FOR ILLUSTRATIVE PURPOSES ONLY AND ARE NOT INTENDED TO COMMEND ANY ONE PARTICULAR DESIGN SOLUTION.

Guidelines for the conversion of barns and oast houses, prepared by the Kent County Council Planning Department.

Oast houses

These distinctive buildings are found in the hop-growing districts of Kent, and parts of Herefordshire, sometimes as part of a farm group but often in open countryside, since the hops had to be dried immediately after having been picked. As the old oast houses are unsuited to modern methods of hop drying many have disappeared, and others have been adapted for new uses. In recent years they have become popular subjects for residential conversion, in spite of the possible inconvenience of the circular rooms in the kilns.

Apart from the kilns, most oast houses had a rectangular storage building attached, and the conversion of these presents similar problems to those of barns and stables. The kilns themselves, most often circular but sometimes square on plan, are generally of brick with conical or high pyramid-shaped roofs, tiled, and capped with timber cowls which turn in the wind. These roofs normally have no openings, and can be completely spoilt by the insertion of domestic style dormer windows, the result of an effort to make maximum use of the available space. This should be avoided, using the roof space for storage only, or perhaps for rooms such as bathrooms, which do not need natural light. Any windows inserted in the walls of the kiln should be tall and narrow, without glazing bars, echoing the narrow ventilation slits sometimes found, and the cowls should be retained. It may be possible to insert some glazing into the cowl to provide a little light in the roof space.

Apart from the simple single oast houses with their attached barns, there are some quite large buildings, incorporating several kilns. Some of these have been converted, quite successfully, into restaurants. Other uses for such buildings could include museums and art galleries, which do not need extensive daylight, craft centres and workshops, and various types of community buildings. These uses, rather than domestic conversion, may well enable the kiln to remain unaltered, at least externally.

Summary

As we have seen, redundant farm buildings can offer considerable scope for conversion, but this needs to be carried out very sympathetically if their simple functional character is not to be lost. This applies not only to the buildings themselves, but to their setting. Where a group of buildings round a farmyard is being converted, the treatment of the floorscape is important. A simple gravel finish is often appropriate, but if something firmer and simpler to maintain is required, plain brick or stone paving, perhaps with some cobbled areas, can look well. Planting is probably best confined to tubs, rather than creating lawns and flower beds. On the buildings, original features such as sack hoists should be allowed to remain, but it is best to avoid creating bogus features of this type, or importing them from elsewhere. The design of any external lighting is also important, simplicity again being the keyword.

The completed scheme at Winfrith Newburgh from the rear (east).

Longcutts Barn, Winfrith Newburgh, Dorset

This barn, of late sixteenth or early seventeenth-century date, is part of a group of cottages and farm buildings, forming an important feature of the village street. They are Grade II listed buildings, and originally belonged to a large local estate. Some years ago the demolition of the whole group was proposed, to provide a road access to a site at the rear, planned for redevelopment by the owners. This scheme was abandoned, and the buildings, with the land at the rear, sold to the local district council. Demolition of the buildings along the street frontage was still proposed, with the land at the rear now allocated for old people's housing. Following local objections, however, an alternative access was provided for the housing site, and the cottages and barn were sold to the Old Buildings Restoration Trust. The council did retain the southern section of the barn for conversion into garages for their own housing scheme.

Farm buildings: case studies

The Trust first restored the cottages, replanning the original four to provide three rather larger units, and these were sold. It was at first hoped that the barn could be restored for some craft or community use, but this did not prove viable and it has now been converted into a single house. The barn was L-shaped in plan, with a main range along the road frontage and a cross-wing at the north (left) end, extending to the rear. It was built of brick, with some interesting diaper patterning in burnt headers, and had a thatched roof. In the north wall of the cross-wing there was evidence that the ground floor had once been open, with the upper walling carried on brick piers, spanned by a large oak lintol, which still survived in the wall. The walling here also incorporated some large pieces of stone, including a length of moulded stone reset in a window cill, which may have come from the nearby ruined abbey at Bindon, demolished at the Dissolution. This cross-wing was divided into two storeys by a timber floor, but the range along the road was open to the roof. In the eighteenth century this range had been extended to the south.

By the time the work started the barn was in poor repair, and part of the roof had collapsed. It was found necessary to renew the whole of the roof structure, and the condition of the gable end walls to the cross-wing was rather unstable. It was considered important to retain, rather than to rebuild, these, and they have been secured to the new roof trusses by a system of diagonal bracing and iron tie rods. The long walls of this wing, which were leaning outwards, have been secured by the insertion of a reinforced concrete ring beam.

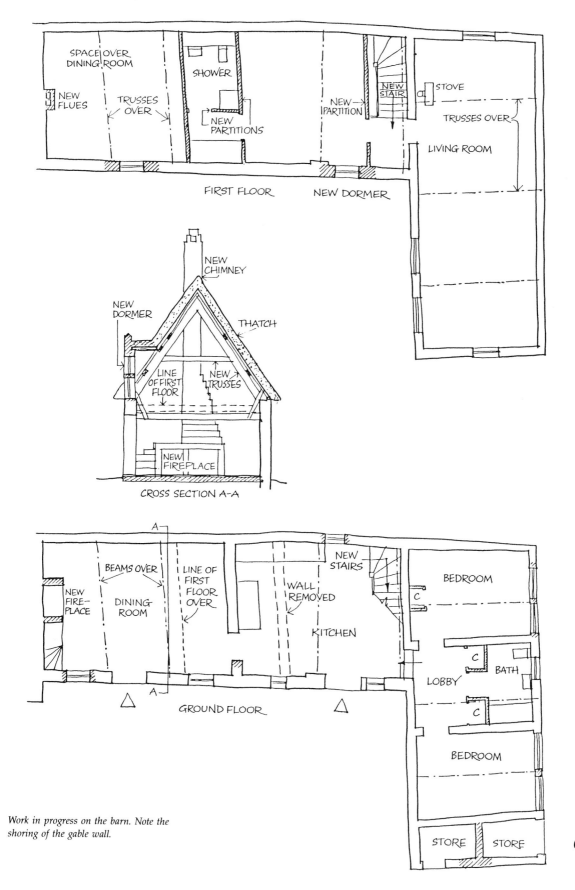

SPACE OVER DINING ROOM

NEW FLUES

TRUSSES OVER

SHOWER

NEW PARTITIONS

NEW PARTITION

NEW STAIR

STOVE

TRUSSES OVER

LIVING ROOM

FIRST FLOOR   NEW DORMER

NEW CHIMNEY

NEW DORMER

THATCH

LINE OF FIRST FLOOR

NEW TRUSSES

NEW FIREPLACE

CROSS SECTION A-A

A

A

BEAMS OVER

LINE OF FIRST FLOOR OVER

WALL REMOVED

NEW STAIRS

BEDROOM

NEW FIRE-PLACE

DINING ROOM

C

KITCHEN

C

BATH

LOBBY

C

GROUND FLOOR

BEDROOM

STORE   STORE

Work in progress on the barn. Note the shoring of the gable wall.

69

View from the main road.

The new staircase.

The conversion scheme has been designed to retain the original character of the barn as far as possible, particularly along the road frontage and the north wall of the cross-wing, which is also visible from the road. In this wall the old wood lintol and the inserted stones have been retained, with the evidence of the old brick piers, and the new windows here are of timber, with plain upright bars, behind which are plain glass sliding panes. On the road front the three new windows are timber casements with lead lights. Similar casements, and two-part stable doors have been inserted in the rear wall. Internally, the upper floor of the cross-wing, which was at rather a low level, has been raised, retaining the original main cross beams, with their joist housings, showing the original floor level. In the range along the road an intermediate floor has been inserted for most of its length, but part of the room at the south end has been left open to the roof, creating a galleried effect. A new timber stair has been inserted, with shaped splat balusters in typical early seventeenth-century style.

Although the roof structure has had to be renewed, a traditional design has been used, and the trusses and rafters are left exposed in the first-floor rooms. One of these is planned as a living room, with a free-standing stove. Two new gabled dormers have been inserted in the rear wall, echoing the design of the gables of the cross-wing, but no dormers have been allowed to break the roof line on the road frontage, or the north slope of the cross-wing. The roof has been rethatched, except for the two dormers at the rear which were tiled,

70

The completed scheme from the southeast. Note the new dormers.

because of problems of weatherproofing due to the steep pitch of the roof and the gable design. A fire-resisting lining has been laid under the thatch. The ground-floor rooms have all been paved with quarry tiles, laid in an interesting broken pattern. This was chosen because few of the rooms are square, and this design involves less cutting of tiles than a normal square layout.

It was originally intended that this building would, like the cottages, be sold on completion of the work, but the Trust has decided to retain and let it, possibly for holiday use. This conversion completes the restoration of an important group of village buildings once threatened with demolition, and has produced an attractive if somewhat unconventional house, which still, at least from the road,

The new floor tiling.

retains much of its agricultural character. The architects were Sell, Wade, Postins of London. The cost of the work (1986) was about £80,000. The Trust obtained a Section 10 Grant from the Department of the Environment.

The north wall, showing evidence of earlier openings, and new windows.

North Barn, Affpuddle, Dorset

This barn, built *c.* 1800, is in an isolated position away from the village, and was probably originally a field barn, dating from the enclosure of open downland for arable farming and grazing. East Farm, Affpuddle, to which it belongs, is within the village, and although the earliest part of the present farmhouse dates from the seventeenth century it is probably on the site of a medieval farm, of pre-enclosure date.

North Barn, which is a prominent feature of the landscape, was built of a mixture of cob, flint and rubble stone, with some brick repairs, and had a hipped thatched roof. There were projecting cart

73

Re-thatching in progress.

porches roughly in the centre of each of the long walls, one with a hipped roof, and one with a lean-to roof. There were the typical narrow ventilation slits in each wall. The main barn was of six bays. At its south end was an attached outbuilding, of similar construction, but little more than half the height of the main barn; this may have been a stable or cart shed. The roof of the main barn was of simple collar-beam form.

The barn stood at the rear of a yard or enclosure, roughly triangular in plan, surrounded by a cob wall, part of which had been rebuilt in concrete blocks, and a further section had collapsed at the time the conversion work started. The capping to this wall, originally thatched, had been largely replaced with tiles.

In its isolated position the barn was being used less and less, and inevitably suffered from lack of maintenance. The son of the owner of East Farm, who wanted a house in the area, therefore decided to convert the barn for this purpose. The barn was listed and so it was necessary to obtain listed building consent, as well as planning permission for change of use. This was not entirely straightforward. The creation of a new residential unit in this isolated position was contrary to local planning policy, and the fact that the entrance to the enclosure was on a bend in the road meant there were difficulties in meeting the requirements of the highway authority. Eventually, however, permission was granted on the grounds that this seemed the best way of preserving the listed building. The planning committee, too, was impressed with the quality of the proposed design.

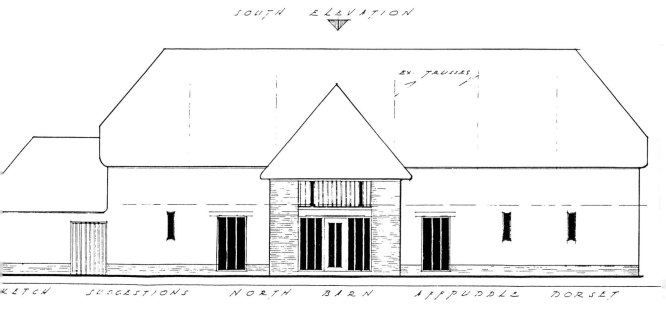

SOUTH ELEVATION

KETCH SUGGESTIONS NORTH BARN AFFPUDDLE DORSET

Sketch elevations for North Barn,
Affpuddle; the west elevation shown to a
larger scale.

WEST ELEVATION

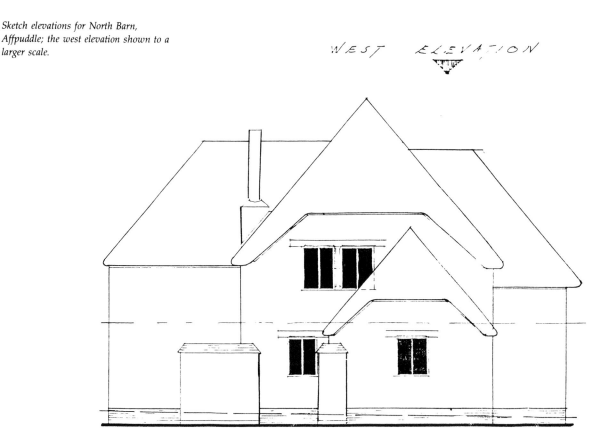

Work in progress on the interior.

Having seen many old barns changed out of all recognition by domestic conversions, the owner was anxious to avoid this approach and to alter the building as little as possible. In order to make full use of the space available, and to avoid any additions, it was decided to insert an intermediate floor. Fortunately the height of the barn allowed this to be done without any need to alter the roof structure. On the ground floor a largely open plan was adopted, with a combined living-kitchen area taking up most of the building. At the north end two bedrooms were partitioned off, and a utility room and cloakroom were fitted into the existing outbuilding at the south end. In the centre, between the two cart porches, an open well has been left in the upper floor, to reveal the full height of the barn, and on the first floor the area round this well has been treated as an open gallery. Two new spiral staircases give access to the upper floor. In the northern section of the barn, the first floor comprises one large bedroom, separated from the gallery by a curtain only. In the southern section two more bedrooms and a bathroom have been partitioned off, while the upper parts of the two cart porches contain another bedroom and a bathroom respectively. In order to obtain sufficient headroom here the lean-to cart porch roof has been raised and given a hipped roof to match the other, this being the main external alteration.

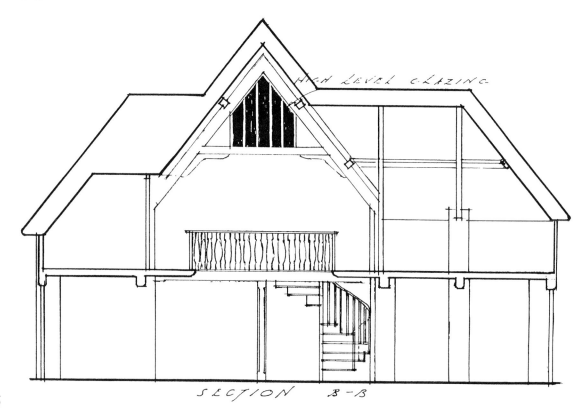

SECTION B-B

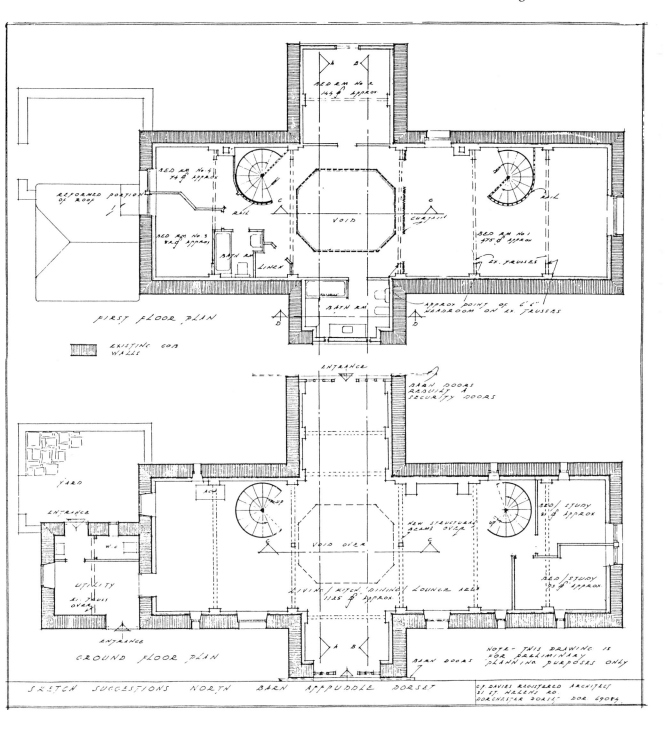

FIRST FLOOR PLAN

EXISTING COB WALLS

GROUND FLOOR PLAN

SKETCH SUGGESTIONS NORTH BARN AFFPUDDLE DORSET

NOTE- THIS DRAWING IS FOR PRELIMINARY PLANNING PURPOSES ONLY

G.F. DAVIES REGISTERED ARCHITECT
31 ST. HELENS RD.
DORCHESTER DORSET DOR 69084

The roof has been kept free from inserted dormers. It was possible to insert a few new windows under the eaves, one in an old opening, to light the upper floor. Internally, some borrowed light was devised at high level in the upper parts of partitions. On the ground floor the lower parts of the original cart entrances have been glazed, incorporating fully glazed doors. The old ventilation slits have been glazed, and a few new windows inserted. These have been kept deliberately simple and barn-like, rather than domestic in character. The upper parts of the cart entrances have been filled with boarding, with some unobtrusive glazing. The roof has been rethatched, and a certain amount of repair has had to be carried out to the roof timbers. New ceiling boarding has been fixed to the undersides of the rafters, leaving the trusses and purlins exposed. The owner wanted an open fire, and an internal chimney has been built against one of the long walls, finished externally with a plain flue pipe.

In order to avoid putting additional loads on to the old walls, and to solve the problems of rising and penetrating damp, a complete inner skin of insulated concrete blocks has been built up, lining the external walls. This gives the interior rather a modern appearance, but it is probably inevitable when a building of this type is converted for residential use, and must be made to comply with modern standards of stability and freedom from damp. In general, though, this scheme is successful, showing a sensitive approach, and a real effort to retain the character of the barn.

The work was carried out by the owner, employing various craftsmen on a direct labour basis. The architect was C.F. Davies of Dorchester.

The original roof structure.

The barn after conversion.

View of the main barn from the courtyard.

Berehayes Farm, Whitchurch Canonicorum, Dorset

This was a farm complex in the centre of the village, near the church, and it was owned by the church until 1946. The farm buildings formed a quadrangle, complete except for an access opening adjoining the road, on the north, and the farmhouse was attached to the rear (south) range, extending eastwards from it. The house dated from *c.* 1500, and was built of the local stone, with a slate roof replacing the original thatch. It retained a number of original features, including a fine oak pointed-arched doorway.

Within the farmyard, the west range comprised the main barn, and there were cowsheds and stables in the north, east and south ranges. These buildings were mainly of stone, with some brick repairs, and may once have been thatched, but the roofs had been replaced with corrugated sheeting, and the main barn had lost its original roof structure and been reduced in height.

By 1983 the buildings had ceased to be used for agricultural purposes and, with the house and eight acres of pasture, were bought by the present owner, a mechanical engineer, who wanted to convert them into holiday accommodation. In spite of the fact that such a use appeared to be in accordance with the County Structure Plan, there was some local opposition to the application for change of use, due largely to fear that the scheme would create a

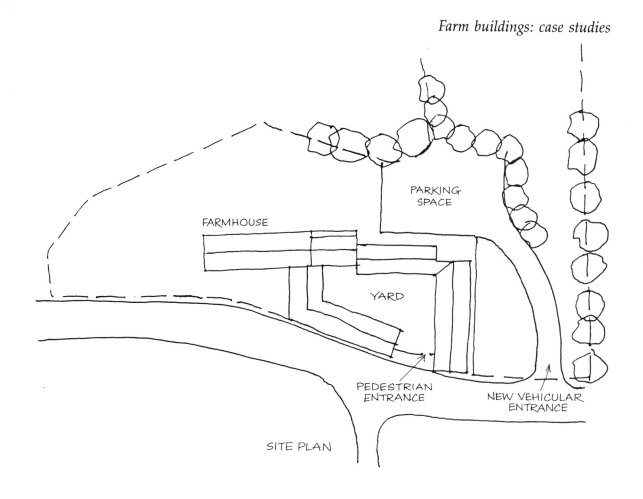

SITE PLAN

ELEVATION OF BARN

The courtyard, looking east.

noise nuisance in the area, and that the local drainage services would be inadequate for the increase in occupation. Eventually, however, planning permission was granted, and the scheme received support and financial assistance from the West Country Tourist Board.

The owner was anxious to preserve and enhance the character of the buildings, and he has restored the original thatched roof of the farmhouse, which is now his home. He also planned to restore the main barn to its original height and to rethatch it. This meant obtaining a relaxation of the Building Regulations, since the barn adjoined the boundary of the site, and it was proposed to divide it into three holiday cottages. The new thatched roof has been given a fire-resisting lining.

The north and south ranges needed some reconstruction, and for this an artificial stone has been used. This, although a reasonable match for the old stone, does look rather raw while it is newly built (1988), but will probably weather down. The roof of the south range has been slated, but the corrugated asbestos has been left on the

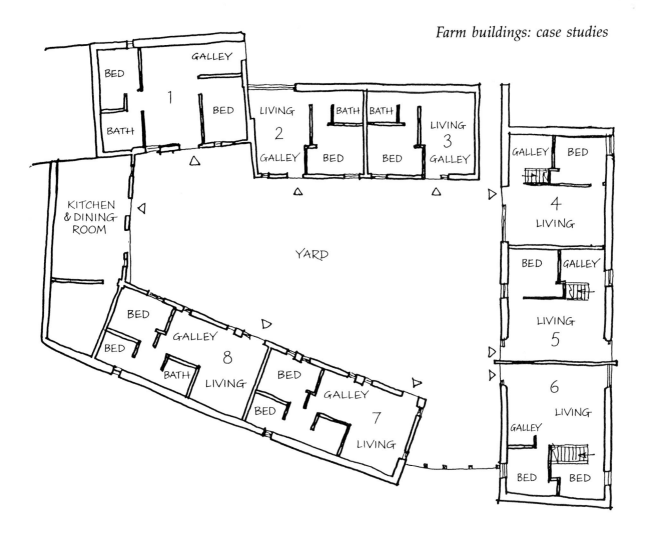

north range, adjoining the road, the aim being to alter the appearance of this as little as possible.

In the main barn the old cart entrances have been given new hipped thatched roofs, and the openings filled largely with glazing. An intermediate first floor has been inserted, but the roof has been kept free from dormers except for a very small 'eyebrow' dormer in the outer, west, face. The few new windows on the ground floor are simple vertical openings, echoing the traditional ventilation slits. This barn now contains three cottages, each with an open living-kitchen area and one, or two, bedrooms on the ground floor, and two bedrooms and a bathroom on the first floor. Along the long east and west walls the first floor has been set back, to allow parts of the living areas to be open to the roof, retaining something of the character of the original barn.

The north range now contains two single-storey cottages, each with a living-kitchen area, two bedrooms and a bathroom. No new openings have been inserted in the north wall (facing the road), thus

The outer face of the main barn.

helping to preserve the appearance of a farm building. The new openings facing the farmyard are tall and narrow, extending from floor to eaves level.

In the south range, the section nearest the house, at the east end, forms one two-bedroomed cottage, with similar tall, narrow windows and a door facing the farmyard. Roof lights have been inserted to provide additional natural lighting. The western section of this range, which is roofed at a slightly lower level, contains two one-bedroom cottages, again with similar doors and windows. All the new doors and windows are of dark stained timber. The east range, which has been little altered, is used as a kitchen and dining area since, although the cottages are self-catering units, a main meal can be provided for tenants.

The old farmyard is finished in coarse gravel, with some old farm implements displayed, and wooden seats against the walls. The old access to the yard from the road has been closed to vehicles, and a new access has been formed to the west of the complex, with car parking arranged unobtrusively at the rear. The cottages are let throughout the year, and appear to be popular. There has been a real effort, largely successful, to retain the appearance of a farmyard. The architect was J.C. Chase of Farnborough, Hampshire.

RIGHT *View from the road. Note the new roof lights.*

Bridgeacre, Uploders, Loders, Dorset

Uploders Place, Uploders, was a farm of pre-enclosure origin, with the farmhouse and barns in the village street. In recent years the farm was split up, the original house being divided into two units and a former stable converted into a separate house, now called Bridgeacre. A large barn adjoining the road was shared by two owners, one being Mr Sanctuary, the owner of Bridgeacre. Since passing out of agricultural use this barn has been used mainly as a garage and store.

This barn, of eighteenth-century date, is built of stone, with a slate roof, and has rather an unusual double-pile plan, consisting of two adjoining ranges under a single-span low pitched roof, the spine wall being carried up to the ridge. It is not clear whether this represents the original design, or whether it is an enlargement of a more conventional single-pile building. There is a central through-way, with large cart entrances in the centres of the long walls. This through-way, and the whole of the outer range adjoining the road, extends for the full height of the building, the rear range having an intermediate floor. On the road frontage there are ventilation slits and holes in the stone walling, while in the rear wall, facing the original farmyard, there are pigeon holes in the upper part of one wall, suggesting that this section was once a pigeon loft.

The owner of Bridgeacre wanted to make better use of his (the larger) part of the barn, converting it into a lettable workshop. The plan was to convert the upper part of the outer range into a workshop, with car parking space below. Only one side of this range belonged to Mr Sanctuary, but a similar scheme is currently being considered for the other side. In the inner range, all of which belonged to Mr Sanctuary, one side was planned as a workshop for

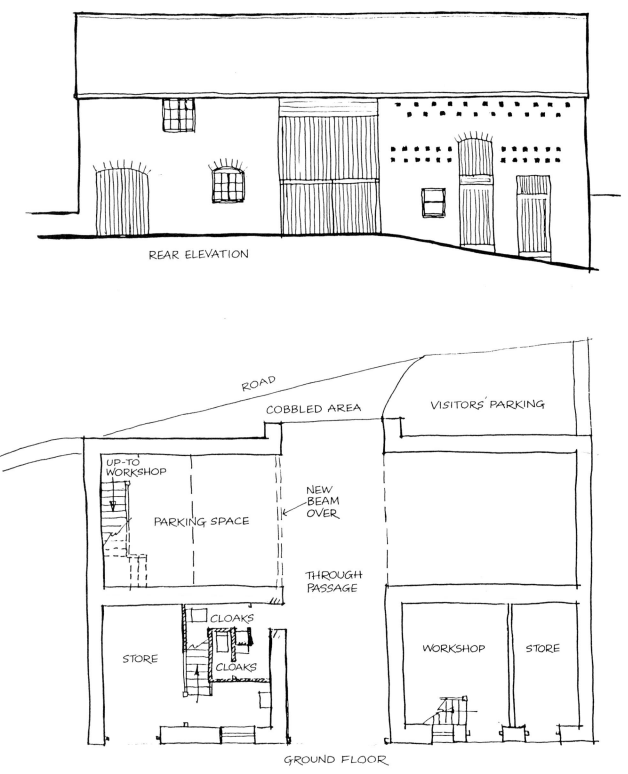

REAR ELEVATION

ROAD

COBBLED AREA

VISITORS' PARKING

UP-TO WORKSHOP

PARKING SPACE

NEW BEAM OVER

THROUGH PASSAGE

CLOAKS

CLOAKS

STORE

WORKSHOP

STORE

GROUND FLOOR

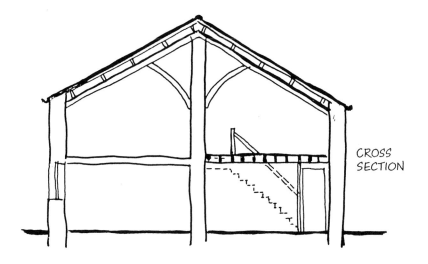

CROSS
SECTION

Interior, the through-way.

his own use, while the other was planned with cloakrooms on the ground floor, to serve the new workshop, and a store above it. This scheme involved inserting a new first floor in the outer range, with an access stair.

Since the village was in a rural development area the scheme was supported by the Council for Small Industries in Rural Areas, who gave advice and prepared plans, and it was assisted by a grant from the Development Commission. There were a few problems in connection with the application for planning permission for change of use, mainly on highway grounds. The barn is sited on a fairly tight bend in the road, and in order to obtain adequate visibility for vehicles entering and leaving the building, part of an old boundary wall had to be taken down. It was a condition of the planning permission that there should be no retail sales from the site, as this could attract more traffic, and restrictions were also placed on the number of vehicles using the building. In order to comply with the Building Regulations the internal walls and ceilings had to be given fire-resisting linings.

In order to light the first-floor workshop, roof lights have been inserted, but because of the fairly shallow roof pitch these are not too obtrusive. The upper parts of the old cart entrances, and the new inner wall between the workshop and the through-way, have been finished with painted timber boarding. On the rear elevation a few new windows have been inserted, but in general the building has not been greatly altered externally.

The cost of the work up to 1986, including repairs, was about £20,000. The Development Commission grant was £6,500. This is

87

View from the courtyard.

a simple scheme, but it shows how a redundant farm building can be adapted to provide local employment, at a reasonable cost and without losing its basic character.

Interior of the first-floor workshop.

Hyde House and Barn, Winchester, Hampshire

These buildings adjoin the site of the former Hyde Abbey, which was destroyed at the Dissolution, and incorporate some re-used abbey materials. The house, set at right-angles to the road, was of late seventeenth or early eighteenth-century date, of brick, with a tiled roof, and was of two storeys. The end wall adjoining the road had a Flemish style gable, and a doorway in a classical style surround. The south wall, facing a courtyard, had another, simpler doorway, and sash windows on each floor. On the north side (the rear) were a short projecting wing and a single-storey lean-to.

The barn, parallel to the road and set back from it at the rear of the courtyard, was of eighteenth-century date, built of stone, with a tiled roof. On the west front, facing the courtyard, were three hipped-roofed projections, possibly of later date. At some period the barn had been used as a maltings, and two large brick kilns survived at the south end. In the centre, north of the projections, was a wide through-way, with double doors in the east and west walls.

The buildings, in the Hyde Conservation Area, had been bought by the city council in conjunction with a redevelopment scheme for the area, incorporating old people's housing and a hostel for the local art school, built in the 1970s. The council was, therefore, faced with the problem of finding a suitable use for the house and barn, which made an important group in the centre of the new development, and, historically, formed a link with the vanished abbey.

Since the early 1960s there have been large-scale excavations in the city, producing a considerable amount of archaeological and documentary material—far more than could be satisfactorily accommodated in the existing museum. The council therefore decided to adapt Hyde House and Barn as a historic resources centre, to house

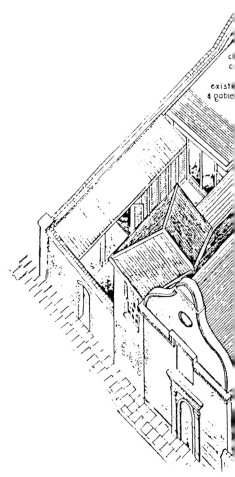

HISTORIC RESOURCES CENTRE
FOR THE CITY OF WINCHESTER MUSEUM
Axonometric Projection showing Details of Conversion and Repairs to the Fabric

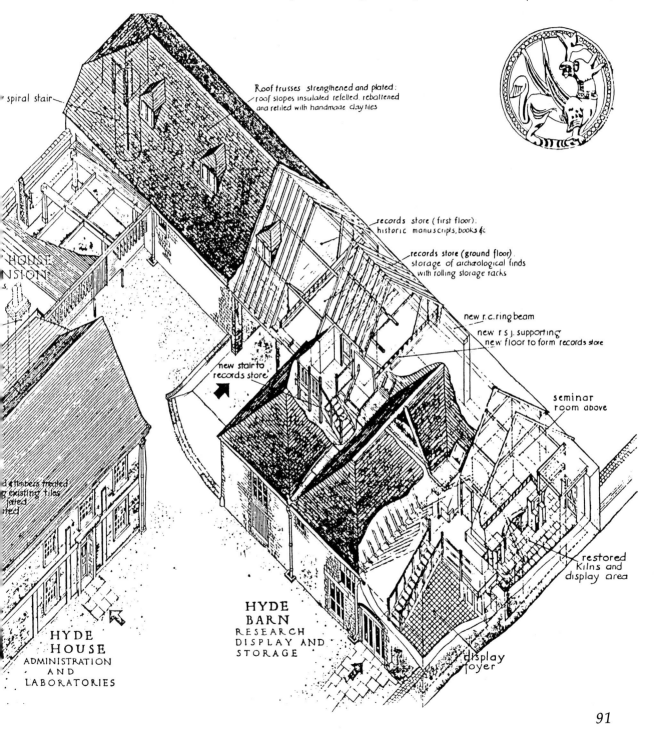

spiral stair

Roof trusses strengthened and plated: roof slopes insulated refelted, rebattened and retiled with handmade clay tiles

HOUSE NSION s.

records store (first floor). historic manuscripts, books &c

records store (ground floor). storage of archæological finds with rolling storage racks

new r.c. ring beam

new r.s.j. supporting new floor to form records store

new stair to records store

seminar room above

d timbers treated g existing tiles ated ted

restored kilns and display area

HYDE HOUSE
ADMINISTRATION
AND
LABORATORIES

HYDE BARN
RESEARCH
DISPLAY AND
STORAGE

display foyer

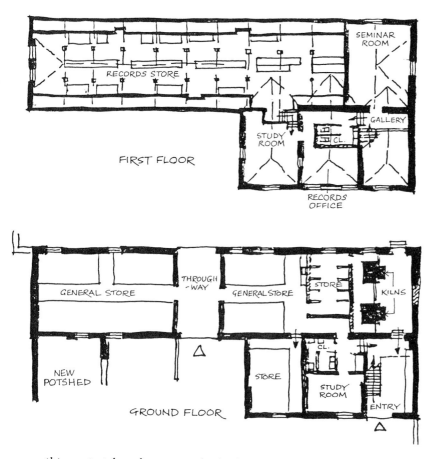

FIRST FLOOR

SEMINAR ROOM

RECORDS STORE

GALLERY

STUDY ROOM

CL.

RECORDS OFFICE

GENERAL STORE

THROUGH-WAY

GENERAL STORE

STORE

KILNS

CL.

NEW POTSHED

STORE

STUDY ROOM

ENTRY

GROUND FLOOR

this material and to provide facilities for students and research workers.

Both buildings needed extensive repairs. In the house, the roofs were stripped and retiled, the roof timbers being repaired and insulation provided. The brickwork was repaired and pointed. The internal joinery, including some good panelling, was repaired, missing features being replaced. The ground floor now contains offices, laboratories, cloakrooms and stores, while the first floor houses further offices and a large drawing office. A new building has been constructed, linking the house to the barn, for cleaning pottery recovered from the excavations. In the barn, the roof has been stripped and retiled, and considerable timber repairs were necessary. The stone walls have been repaired and pointed, and a reinforced concrete ring beam has been inserted at eaves level to stabilise the structure. New doors and windows were inserted in the existing openings. Internally, there has been substantial remodelling to suit the new use, and the first-floor timbers have been renewed, creating more convenient ceiling heights. The southernmost of the three projections has been turned into an entrance hall, with a new staircase, and a gallery at first-floor level. The central projection contains a study room and cloakrooms, and most of the rest of the ground floor is used for the storage of archaeological material, with

The restored kiln, now used as a display area.

92

The barn after conversion.

Part of the barn before conversion.

Interior one of the first-floor rooms.

specially made storage units. The old malt kilns have been restored, forming the main features of a display area, with facilities for public viewing. On the first floor are further stores, in this case mainly for records, a study room and a seminar room for students. The open timber roofs have been exposed to view wherever practicable, and in the building generally various fragments of carved stone from the abbey, found built into the walls, have been reset as features.

In order to comply with Fire Precautions requirements, some ceilings have had to be lined, but the main beams have been left exposed. New fire-resisting doors, of traditional vertical battened design, have been used throughout the barn. The converted buildings now form a valuable addition to the city's museums and record office. Although not intended to be open to the public as a museum, they do provide good facilities for students, as well as adequate and suitable accommodation for archaeological finds and records—features lacking in many museums where space is at a premium. This use also has the advantage of requiring minimum alterations to the buildings. Eventually it is hoped to restore the nearby abbey gateway—the only surviving standing structure— and put it to a suitable use. The Centre was opened in 1981, the cost of the work having been about £290,000. The architects were Donald Insall and Associates of London.

93

6 Windmills and watermills

Windmills and watermills, some of our earliest industrial buildings, once played an important part in the rural economy. Since the end of the nineteenth century, competition from large-scale commercial milling has meant that most of them ceased working, and many that have not been demolished have been converted for other purposes. In recent years, though, with the growing demand for stone-ground flour, there has been a revival of interest in traditional milling, so that a number of both windmills and watermills have been restored. In some cases this has been primarily as museum pieces, or tourist attractions, but a few are working on a genuinely commercial basis. This trend may grow, but many mills are still being offered for sale for conversion to new uses.

Windmills

These are of three types. First the post mill, always of timber-framed construction, where the mill structure housing the machinery is supported on a post fixed to the ground. The mill has to be turned to face the wind, and in the earliest examples this was done by hand, using a raking pole at the rear of the structure. Later, the fantail was invented, a small fanned wheel which turned the mill automatically as the wind changed. Another later development was the round-house, a circular brick or stone structure built around the lower part of the post, below the mill structure, thus protecting the post from the weather and providing storage space.

The second type was the tower mill, a solid construction of brick or stone, of which only the timber-framed cap, carrying the sails, was turned into the wind by the fantail. The third type, the smock mill, was similar, but was built of timber framing, and weather-boarded. It was named from a supposed resemblance to a shepherd's smock.

Most windmills had four sails, but occasionally five or more are found. The earliest sails were of open timber framing, covered with canvas, like the sails of a ship. Later, the patent shuttered sail was invented, the shutters functioning like those of a Venetian blind. Only when the sails were covered with the canvas, or the shutters closed, would the sails turn in the wind and work the machinery.

A windmill at Rye, Sussex, converted and extended to form a hotel.

95

Windmills and watermills

Once a mill stopped working, the sails were generally the first things to decay. Sometimes they have survived more or less intact, but often only the stocks, or central timber members, remain. In other cases they have disappeared completely. Indeed, after many years of disuse and lack of maintenance, the cap of a tower mill may well have perished, and a post mill is unlikely to have survived, although many of the round-houses remain, their original function often forgotten.

When it comes to a question of conversion, it must be admitted that it is difficult to see any practical new use for a post mill, which should perhaps be thought of more as a piece of machinery than a building. If it has survived in a condition to justify restoration, such a mill is probably best treated as a museum piece, and as such it could well become a tourist attraction. The round-house could become an information centre, a shop, or a small workshop.

The more substantial brick and stone tower mills offer more possibilities for conversion, although if the machinery has survived it will take up most of the interior. Since so many mills have been lost, and in view of the revived interest in milling, it is most unfortunate when, in order to adapt the building for a new use, all the machinery is removed. Indeed, there may well be opposition from the planning authority to any scheme involving this. When a mill is substantially complete, the aim should always be to restore it, if not to commercial working then as an important relic of the past, and a potential tourist attraction.

In many cases, though, most or all of the machinery will have been removed, or be in such a poor state that restoration is not practicable, and in these cases one can consider other uses for the building. No machinery, however fragmentary, should be destroyed. It could well be used to help restore other mills. The local planning authority, or a local historical or amenity society, may be able to help find a suitable new home for any unwanted machinery, or mill stones.

Tower mills have been converted for a number of uses. Their siting is of course important, as they may be found either in or near villages, or in quite isolated positions. Apart from the more usual corn grinding mills, they were also used for pumping water for drainage purposes, and some of these have survived in the Fens and on the Norfolk Broads. For residential use, the problems are not unlike those arising with oast houses, their design really allowing for one circular room on each floor. In order to form a workable house it is often necessary to build extensions, unless there are some existing outbuildings which can be used. Any extensions will need very careful design, and should be kept as simple as possible. Single-storey buildings of modest size, and with pitched roofs, or traditional construction, will generally be most appropriate. Conversion for holiday use may well be better than for full-time occupation, as fewer alterations will probably be needed. Tower mills generally

Windmill between Shepshed and Ashby, near Loughborough, extended and converted to a house. The two surviving sails were retained. See p. 2-3.

have windows on each floor, and these should if possible be retained without enlargement, or additions. One problem likely to arise under the Building Regulations is that the converted tower will probably contain more than two storeys. This will mean that the staircases may have to be enclosed, encroaching on the already limited floor space, and perhaps detracting from the character of the interior; the original ladder-type stairs are unlikely to be accepted. There may also be problems with the fire-resistance of the floors, and an early consultation with the local building control officer is advisable.

Other possible uses are as offices or workshops, perhaps incorporating a shop on the ground floor, a museum or interpretation centre. Here again, problems with the Building Regulations must be anticipated, and for any public use the limited space on each floor may make it difficult to provide efficient and safe circulation. Smock mills may be converted in similar ways, but, being timber-framed and weatherboarded, they are (as we have seen with some farm buildings) likely to need additional weatherproofing and insulation for most uses.

Whatever new use is chosen, the cap of a tower mill should be restored to its original form, and any surviving sails or stocks retained. If the sails are missing a decision will have to be taken on whether to restore them, even though they will not be used. They will certainly add to the character of the finished building, as well as to its maintenance costs! If, though, it is decided to restore the sails, these should be authentic copies of the original ones, as anything less will devalue the whole building. It may be necessary to arrange for the cap to be turned into the wind by a fantail, or to have some other means of avoiding damage by tail-winding, and the advice of a skilled millwright should be obtained.

The watermill at Bickleigh, Devon, now a crafts centre and museum.

Watermills

Watermills generally have a greater potential for conversion than windmills. They vary greatly in size, type and construction. On the humblest scale we find the small country corn mill, serving a village community, sometimes combined with a bakery and a miller's house. In towns there are larger mills, and, particularly in some parts of the country, mills used for purposes other than grinding corn. Water power was used for fulling and other textile processes, and for smelting metal, as in the hammer mills serving the Sussex ironworks and the Cornish tin industry. At the other end of the scale are the large early textile mills of Yorkshire and Lancashire, originally water-powered. These last, really factories, will be looked at in another chapter. It is interesting to note that mills sometimes changed their function; a corn mill might for a time become a flax mill, and then revert to corn grinding as local economic circumstances altered.

The smaller rural and urban mills were built of the local available materials, stone, brick and weatherboarded timber-framing all being found. They were mostly of two or three storeys, plus a loft containing the grain hoppers. These lofts often had mansard roofs, to provide the maximum headroom. The water wheel was generally outside the mill, but was sometimes incorporated within the structure. In the late nineteenth and early twentieth centuries the wheels were sometimes replaced by the more efficient turbines.

When a mill stopped working, the machinery was sometimes removed and sold either for scrap or for use in another mill, but often it was left, and some mills now being sold for conversion are found to contain a complete, or practically complete, set of machinery, together with old tools and, occasionally, old accounts and other records. These last can be of considerable historic interest

A large windmill at Winchester, converted to flats.

99

and should never be destroyed. If the new owner does not want to keep them they should be offered to the local record office. As with windmills, if the machinery is largely complete it should be kept in-situ. The current revival of interest in milling means that there are many people anxious to acquire and restore a mill to working order, and this should be the first choice when considering the future of the building. The Wind and Watermill Section of the Society for the Protection of Ancient Buildings (for address, see Appendix III) can often help to find a potential new miller, particularly if the mill house, or another nearby house, is available. Again as with windmills, there may well be opposition from the local planning authority to any scheme which involves stripping out sound, or restorable, material from a mill. This need not necessarily preclude some other use for the building, since, except in the smallest mills, the machinery does not always occupy the whole of the floor area; storage space was also incorporated.

Sometimes, though, we shall find that all or most of the machinery has gone, and the remainder is too fragmentary, or in too poor a state, to justify a full restoration. Even in these cases, though, machinery should not be destroyed. If it cannot be left in place it may be possible to use it in another mill. As with windmills, the Society for the Protection of Ancient Buildings, the local authority, or a local historical or amenity society should be offered any machinery or stones. Whatever new use is chosen, the water wheel should be kept if it is in reasonable repair, or capable of repair, particularly if it is on the outside of the mill. It provides evidence of the origin of the building, and its retention normally presents fewer maintenance problems than does that of the sails of a windmill.

West Mill, Bridport, converted to an architect's office. Most of the machinery was retained, and the turbine has been restored to working order.

Flatford Mill, made famous by Constable's painting, now houses a Field Study Centre.

Before we look at possible uses for watermills, a few words of caution should be given to prospective purchasers. First, anyone buying a watermill may find himself responsible for the maintenance, and perhaps the operation when necessary, of the hatches and sluices. Next, the possible danger of flooding must not be overlooked, and this could affect the use of the ground floor. It may be possible to obtain local information about flood levels over the last decade or so. Then any future plans by the water authority such as flood prevention schemes could affect the water level in the river and/or mill race. This could be particularly important if it is hoped to operate the machinery, or even to be able to turn the wheel. A permanent change in the water level might even affect the foundations of the building—some mills are built out into the river or mill race. It is, therefore, important to consult the local water authority or river board before deciding on the purchase, or future use, of a watermill. If the original use has lapsed, and it is planned to revive it, a charge may be payable for the necessary permission from the water authority.

Assuming that these problems can be overcome, let us look at possible uses for watermills. These will depend on the size, construction and location of the buildings. Residential conversion is popular, and many mills have been made into attractive houses. This can include holiday use which, as we have seen in other cases, may need less drastic alterations than does conversion for full-time occupation. Other mills have been converted into restaurants, workshops, shops, museums and interpretation centres, and for various community uses. Some larger mills have been successfully

converted into youth hostels, blocks of flats and suites of offices or workshops.

Although some of the problems of converting watermills are similar to those met with in farm buildings, there are some more specific ones which should be borne in mind. First, as with farm buildings, the timber-framed and weatherboarded mills will probably need additional weatherproofing and insulation. Some of the existing ceiling heights may be rather low. Recent amendments to the Building Regulations make this less of a problem than it once was, but in, for instance, a residential conversion, it is often best to plan such rooms as bathrooms, utility rooms and stores on these floors, even if this results in a less conventional layout. It is generally inadvisable to take out existing floors, especially in a timber-framed building, because of the consequent risk of structural movement and possible damage. In most watermills there is a good deal of exposed timberwork—ceilings were rarely plastered—and this can cause problems with the fire regulations, particularly for any public use or, indeed, for residential use if the resultant house has more than two storeys. The existing stairs are likely to be very steep, little better than ladders, and will not comply with the Building Regulations. When new stairs are to be inserted, they should be kept simple in character. Sometimes a spiral stair is suitable and saves floor space. Recent amendments to the Building Regulations have made it easier to use these. It may be possible to leave the old stairs in position, in addition to any new one required, and this can be an advantage in a large or unconventionally planned building.

For certain new uses it may be found necessary to strengthen the floors in order to comply with the Building Regulations. This may

LEFT *and* ABOVE *A mill and maltings at Salisbury, Wiltshire, has been made the nucleus of a new shopping precinct. Note the former mill race at the right end of the smaller picture* (RIGHT).

Littlebourne Mill, Kent, converted to a house. The alterations and additions have retained the 'industrial' character of the building.

RIGHT *and* BELOW *Walford Mill, Wimborne, Dorset. This mill had lost all its machinery, having been used as a builder's workshop. It has now been repaired and is in use as a crafts centre. The chimney was built for a steam engine which had replaced the old waterwheel. Note the new brick paving, appropriate to the building.*

seem strange, as they will probably originally have carried heavy loads of grain or flour, and had to withstand the vibration of the mill machinery. However, the local authority will probably require calculations proving that the floor is capable of carrying the prescribed loads for the particular use, and this is not always easy with traditional construction.

As with farm buildings, the existing windows and doors should be retained, unaltered if possible, and additional openings avoided. To provide additional daylight if required without altering the character of the building, or weakening the structure, glazing can sometimes be incorporated into a loft door, or the lucarne (the dormer above the sack hoist).

As we have seen, many watermills have steeply pitched, or mansard, roofs, providing substantial lofts, and it is understandable to want to make use of this space, which will originally have been used to house the grain storage hoppers. It may be necessary to remove these, but if possible a section should be retained. In any case, care will have to be taken not to weaken the structure when removing the hoppers, particularly in a timber-framed mill, where they may have some structural function. Great care will be needed in designing any dormers or roof lights, and use should be made of

Harnham Mill, Salisbury, Wiltshire. The building on the right of the picture is medieval in origin, and has become a restaurant, while the adjoining nineteenth-century mill house has been made into an hotel.

*Two watermills converted as restaurants.
ABOVE Cotes Mill, near Loughborough,
has been little altered, and still appears
'industrial' externally. RIGHT The Abbey
Mill, Tewkesbury, has been rather more
smartened up, but retains much of its
character.*

existing openings, or openings in end gable walls, as far as possible.

When a large mill is being converted for some public use, such as a restaurant, it may be possible to retain the machinery, perhaps behind a glass screen, with suitable lighting, making an attractive feature in the building. If this is planned, and particularly if it is proposed to keep the wheel and machinery turning, without actually grinding, the advice of a skilled millwright should be sought. The Society for the Protection of Ancient Buildings may be able to suggest a suitable craftsman.

In a residential conversion, and for some other uses, it may be desired to insert a fireplace in a mill. Sometimes, as we have seen, the mill incorporated a bakery and the existing flues can be used. If this is not the case, a new brick chimney can look rather inappropriate, and, as with farm buildings, a simple metal flue of 'industrial' character may be a better alternative. In some cases there may be an attached mill house, which can make the conversion rather easier. The more conventional rooms can be provided in the house, leaving the mill itself as a general 'open plan' living area, with the minimum of partitioning or other alterations.

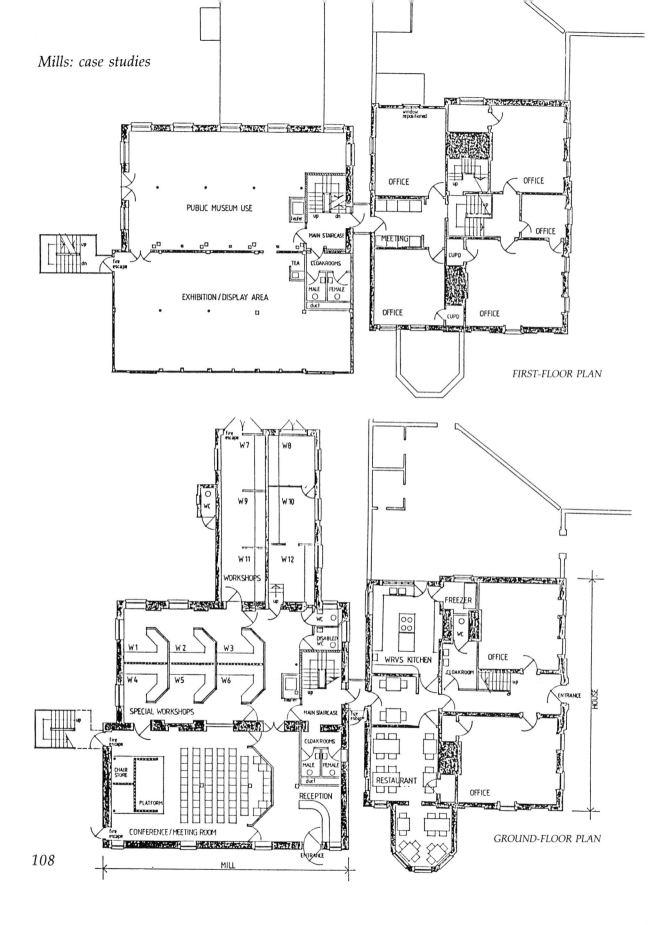

PUBLIC MUSEUM USE

EXHIBITION / DISPLAY AREA

up
dn
fire
escape

window
repositioned

OFFICE

OFFICE

up

OFFICE

MAIN STAIRCASE

MEETING

CUPD

TEA

CLOAKROOMS

MALE

FEMALE

duct

OFFICE

CUPD

OFFICE

FIRST-FLOOR PLAN

fire
escape

W 7

W 8

WC

W 9

W 10

W 11

W 12

WORKSHOPS

up

WC

DISABLED
WC

FREEZER

WC

W 1

W 2

W 3

WRVS KITCHEN

OFFICE

W 4

W 5

W 6

CLOAKROOM

up

SPECIAL WORKSHOPS

up

ENTRANCE

up
fire
escape

MAIN STAIRCASE

fire
escape

HOUSE

CHAIR
STORE

CLOAKROOMS

PLATFORM

MALE

FEMALE

duct

RESTAURANT

OFFICE

fire
escape

CONFERENCE / MEETING ROOM

RECEPTION

ENTRANCE

MILL

GROUND-FLOOR PLAN

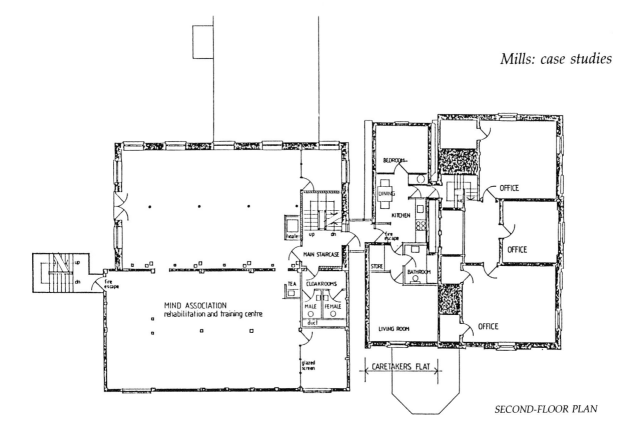

SECOND-FLOOR PLAN

Within the plan:

MIND ASSOCIATION
rehabilitation and training centre

fire escape
up
dn

up
dn

heater

MAIN STAIRCASE

fire escape

BEDROOM

DINING

KITCHEN

OFFICE

OFFICE

STORE

BATHROOM

TEA

CLOAKROOMS

MALE   FEMALE

duct

LIVING ROOM

OFFICE

glazed screen

CARETAKERS FLAT

Moulsham Mill, Chelmsford, Essex

Moulsham Mill, a former watermill, is a prominent landmark on the River Chelmer, at its junction with the Cam, a little way out of the centre of Chelmsford. The earliest records of a mill on this site are found in the Domesday Survey, and through successive rebuildings the mill continued in use until the early 1970s. During the nineteenth century the use of water power was replaced by a steam engine, and roller plant replaced the mill stones, so that no early machinery survived. By the time the mill ceased working it consisted of two attached parallel ranges, each of four storeys, with grain hoppers in the lofts. The earlier, south range, probably of eighteenth-century date, is a timber-framed structure, on a brick base, weatherboarded externally, while the north range, of the nineteenth century but apparently on the foundations of an earlier structure, is of brick, the upper floors of this section being supported on cast iron columns. Attached to the east end is the former mill house, an attractive eighteenth-century building, linked to the mill by an earlier, possibly sixteenth-century, block which may have been the original house. There were various attached outbuildings, mainly timber framed and weatherboarded, and in rather poor repair.

109

Mills: case studies

Although the building was listed, it was by the early 1960s in rather a neglected condition, and superficially dilapidated. The external weatherboarding had deteriorated, allowing water to penetrate the structure, and the whole property was rather run down. Listed building consent had been granted for certain alterations, which included the insertion of new windows, and other work to adapt the mill for industrial use, retaining the house as a residence. This permission, however, was not implemented.

In 1983, interest in the mill was expressed by the Church and Community Interface Association (Interface), a charity set up by the Diocese of Chelmsford to promote employment and assist the unemployed by providing training and help in setting up small businesses, working closely with the Manpower Services Commission. It was felt that the restoration of Moulsham Mill could, first, provide employment on the work itself and, after completion, provide accommodation for a number of newly established small firms, for training schemes, and for other community projects.

In 1983, Interface commissioned a full feasibility study on the mill from Architecton, a Bristol firm of architects with considerable experience of this type of work. They went into the matter in considerable detail, investigating the possibility of different uses, the likely problems (for instance, with planning, building and fire regulations), the probable costs and sources of grant aid, and the financial viability of the scheme in terms of running costs. It was in the light of this report that Interface decided to proceed, and a lease at a peppercorn rent was granted by the owners, Messrs W.H. Marriage and Sons, who had owned the mill since 1839. They also contributed £20,000 towards the cost of the work.

Interior of the ground-floor meeting room.

Interior of one of the attic workshops.

The restoration of the mill was carried out under the Manpower Services Commission Community Programme, with a civil engineer as project director. Under this programme, labour costs are paid by the Commission, leaving the sponsor to provide materials. Grants and donations amounted to £15,000. The total cost was £260,000, the Manpower Services Commission contributing £200,000, leaving the balance to be raised by Interface.

Minimum alterations were carried out to the building, particularly to the exterior, apart from the demolition of some of the outbuildings, and the construction of an external fire escape stair at one end of the mill. On an industrial building of this type this stair does not look out of place. A few new windows had to be inserted, but these were designed as inconspicuously as possible. The mill house was converted to offices. In the mill itself the ground floor was planned to provide a reception centre, a conference/meeting room, and some special workshops for training unemployed people in new skills. On the upper floors is a series of small businesses, including a restaurant and several retail outlets—the building being open to the public—while one floor is occupied by the MIND organisation, which assists the mentally handicapped. Certain internal works were necessary in order to comply with the building and fire regulations, but it proved possible to leave many of the timber beams and the timber and cast iron columns exposed, thus retaining the industrial character of the building. Apart from the external fire escape stair, there is an internal stair at the other end of the building. As far as possible, internal divisions between the various users are in the form of screens, thus keeping the original open aspect of the interior.

There is no doubt that the two factors largely contributing to the success of this scheme were, first, the commissioning of a thorough preliminary feasibility study, and, second, the co-operation of the local planning and building control authorities.

111

The Maltings, Sherborne, Dorset, after conversion (for full description see pp. 126-31).

7 Industrial buildings

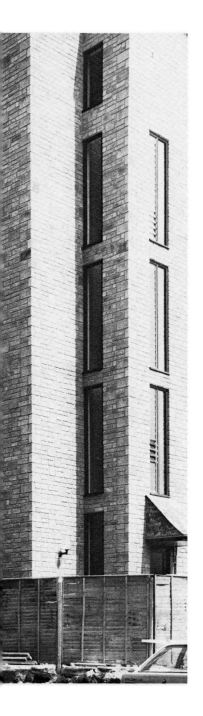

Under this heading I shall be considering a variety of buildings, such as factories, workshops, breweries and maltings, potteries and glassworks, and buildings connected with the transport industries. Sometimes all these are found associated with groups of workers' houses, adding to their historic interest. Most of these buildings date from the later eighteenth, nineteenth and early twentieth centuries.

Industrial buildings may become redundant, and available for conversion, for a number of reasons. In some cases the original use has ceased, or been superseded by new processes for which the old buildings are unsuited, as, for instance, the old style potteries with their bottle kilns. In other cases the use may have expanded to such an extent that the old buildings are no longer large enough to hold them, and there is no room on the site for expansion. This often happens in town centres, where old-established industries tend to move out to new trading estates on the outskirts of the town, selling their old sites, which probably have a high potential development value. In some cases, sadly, the buildings become redundant as a result of a general economic decline in the area. Buildings associated with the canals and railways have suffered from the decline of these transport systems.

It often seems that while any plans for town centre redevelopment which involve the demolition of houses or public buildings of some architectural merit, are scrutinised and often opposed by the public, the fate of industrial buildings has until recently aroused far less interest. To return to the Potteries, only with the disappearance of nearly all the old bottle kilns was it realised that these towns had lost their most distinctive visual features, and an important link with their past.

Today, with a growing interest in industrial archaeology, we are seeing a new attitude to these buildings. Once little appreciated, and even despised as unwelcome reminders of a rather grim phase in our history, it is now realised that they have an austere character which can add to the interest of a street, and that all aspects of our past may well be worth remembering. Quite apart from these considerations, it is now increasingly felt that such substantial buildings should not be lightly destroyed, until the case for their preservation has been fully examined.

LEFT *The Gladstone Pottery Museum is a successful adaptation of one of the few old surviving potteries in Stoke, with its bottle kilns.*

Since industrial buildings vary so much in size, style and construction, it is not surprising that we are now seeing them being converted for a wide variety of uses. With the growing interest in social and industrial history, a number have been successfully converted into industrial museums. Some of these are not simply static displays, but working museums where the old work processes are continued, often with some economic success. At the Gladstone Pottery Museum, at Stoke on Trent, where articles made in the museum workshops are sold to the public, these now provide a substantial part of its income. Such schemes, though, are inevitably limited, and normally only one or two buildings in a town can be preserved in this way. When considering other uses we have to take into account the type of building, its construction and its location.

Certain types of factory, such as the formal, multi-storey textile mills and warehouses, have been successfully converted into flats, suites of offices, or of smaller workshops. For this latter use, financial aid may sometimes be available for schemes designed to promote employment in certain areas (see Chapter 4). These factories were generally very well built, with solid brick or concrete floors,

BELOW *A large warehouse in Worcester, in process of conversion to offices.*

115

providing a high level of fire resistance, although there may be problems with the free-standing cast iron columns often found supporting the floors. The fire regulations will generally require these to be encased, but they are often quite ornamental in character, and it may be desired to leave them exposed. It is sometimes possible to work out an acceptable compromise solution, perhaps by building up solid party walls, so that the floors are no longer technically supported on the columns, which can remain as features in the rooms. As far as sound is concerned, the solid floors will probably provide a good basic standard against airborne sound, but some form of sound-deadening may be necessary against structure-borne sound. This can sometimes be provided by false ceilings or floors, as described later. These buildings are generally of open-plan form over much of the floor area, and can be divided into flats or offices quite easily, but the planning should respect the existing window pattern, which is generally quite regular. In some cases the ceiling heights will be greater than is required, and false ceilings or floors can often be inserted, enabling pipework and other services to be concealed. The existing window pattern should be retained, and wherever possible the existing casements or sashes re-used. They are often of cast iron, which can generally be cleaned

Change of use in Worcester. The two pictures LEFT show Brown's Restaurant, formed from a nineteenth-century riverside warehouse. Note the glazing in the old entrance. ABOVE A former glove factory on the outskirts of the city, recently opened as an hotel — its viability probably helped by its position on a new ring road.

and rustproofed. If it becomes necessary to insert new casements they should be purpose-made to fit the existing openings, and of a simple design, following the original ones as closely as possible. Pseudo-Georgian or other 'domestic' pattern windows will generally look rather out of place.

Some of the early and mid nineteenth-century factories are quite elaborate buildings, in a Gothic or Italianate style, with ornament in contrasting brick, terracotta or stone. Wherever possible this ornament should be kept, and carefully made good where necessary. The tall chimneys are features of many old factories. These are unlikely to have any functional purpose in the converted building, and they do present a maintenance problem. Where possible, though, they should be retained, as they can be important townscape features, punctuating the skyline rather like church spires.

Breweries and maltings can sometimes be converted in similar ways, but a problem peculiar to these buildings is the low ceiling height often found on the malting floors. Recent revisions of the Building Regulations have been helpful in this respect, but even so the headrooms may not be adequate for normal habitable or working rooms. It may be necessary to take out parts of some of the floors, provided that this can be done without weakening the

RIGHT *The old Marconi works in Chelmsford, Essex, have been adapted as offices by the local Water Authority. The manager's house, shown more clearly in the picture on the* LEFT, *has been retained, and new extensions can just be seen,* FAR LEFT.

structure, and form galleried rooms with areas such as bathrooms, cloakrooms and stores in the low-ceilinged areas. A flexible approach to the design of the flats or offices is essential in these cases. What should be avoided is the wholesale removal and renewal of floors at new levels. As well as causing possible structural problems this will almost certainly involve altering the window levels, leaving little of the building intact. Maltings often had kilns projecting above the general roof line, rather like those of oast houses, and these should be retained, as indeed should any significant surviving internal evidence of them. Even if it is not practicable to incorporate these into individual flats or offices, they could form an interesting feature in a common entrance hall.

In towns, industrial buildings of this type are often found adjoining a river, canal or harbour, and full advantage should be taken of this, to enhance the setting of the buildings. Many towns have in the recent past tended to turn their backs on their waterways, but are now beginning to appreciate them and open them up to public view, particularly since the general reduction of water pollution following recent legislation. Some of the early textile mills were water-powered, and may retain one or more water wheels and other early machinery. This should all be retained as far as possible. The earliest of these mills were often in rural areas, and surviving examples in such situations are particularly suitable for conversion into hotels, guest houses, hostels, field study centres, or blocks of holiday flats, subject to local planning policy. In all cases, the aim should be to retain their simple character.

RIGHT *The Town Cellars, Poole, a medieval warehouse, is now the town's maritime museum. The building once extended across the road to the left. Part of the interior is shown* BELOW.

ABOVE *and* BELOW *Warehousing in Gloucester Docks, converted for a variety of uses, including offices for the local council.*

In towns, industrial buildings of less regular and formal design have been converted into shopping complexes, perhaps with flats or offices above the shops. With many buildings of this type, while the original structures are generally quite substantial, they will often have acquired during their working life later additions of poorer quality, and it is sometimes best to remove these, to provide more light and air and external circulation space. The making good of any walls exposed by partial demolition will need careful design, to avoid a makeshift appearance. For any dual or multiple use it will be necessary to provide independent access to the upper floors, separate from that to the shop, and the floors separating the various uses will have to have a high standard of fire resistance and sound insulation. In a shopping precinct it is an advantage if the approach to the shops can be pedestrianised, but it will be necessary to provide for servicing by delivery vehicles. Early consultation with the planning and highway authorities is important.

Many industrial buildings grew up along the canals when they were in commercial use; mills, warehouses, stables for the canal boat

A former canalside warehouse at Hyde, Cheshire, now converted to offices. The old loft doors on each floor have been glazed to give improved lighting in the building.

LEFT *Stockton Brook station, on a now disused railway line near the Calden Canal, is now a shop. The re-opening of the canal for cruising has probably increased the shop's trade.*

horses, canal workers' houses and toll houses. With the decline of the canals these buildings often fell into disrepair, but the revival of the canals for leisure use has brought about the restoration and conversion of many of them.

The railways which replaced the canals are themselves in decline in many areas, and their buildings are becoming redundant. As with the canals, some have been restored to new uses. Stations have been converted into houses, shops and restaurants, the use depending largely on their location. Such conversions normally present few problems. The buildings are often acquired by enthusiasts, only too anxious to preserve their character. A number of former railway lines have been converted to footpaths or cycle tracks, and in these cases the buildings may be given a new lease of life as shelters, cafés, information centres and hostels.

I have stressed the importance of maintaining the character of these industrial buildings, and resisting the temptation to 'over-domesticate' them. This applies to the setting as well as the buildings themselves, and as with farm buildings a suburban style garden layout is best avoided. It may be possible to re-use old stone or brick pavings, cobbles or setts, but if these have not survived appropriate new materials should be selected.

Even in towns where the centres have been largely rebuilt the value of the surviving early industrial buildings is now, rather belatedly, being appreciated, providing as they do a foil to the blandness of much of the new development.

The Old Needlemakers and Old Candlemakers, Lewes, Sussex

This was a redundant industrial building in the centre of Lewes, such as is found in many towns, in rather a run-down condition, and of which many examples have been demolished in town centre redevelopment schemes, or to provide car parks. This building dated from the early to mid nineteenth century, and was originally a candle factory. This use continued until early in the present century, when the factory closed and the last box of candles to be made there was given to the local museum. The building then went through a number of industrial uses. In the First World War part of it was used for making surgical needles.

The factory consisted of a long rectangular range, of two storeys, with lofts in the roof space. The walls were of brick, and the roof partly slated and partly pantiled, one section having been replaced with corrugated iron. Although the building was not of any great intrinsic architectural merit, it was a prominent feature of the area, and of some local historic interest, being a relic of one of the town's old industries. By the 1970s it had fallen into disuse and was in a

RIGHT *Interior of the first-floor shopping area, and* BELOW *the exterior, showing the new roof lights and the old chimney stack.*

semi-derelict state. At this point it was bought by the district council for demolition, to provide an enlarged car park.

This proposal attracted some local opposition. In spite of the poor condition of the building and the lack of any foreseeable use for it, the local amenity society pressed for its retention. Although not listed, it was in the Conservation Area and, since the building belonged to the council, the consent of the Secretary of State for the Environment was needed for its demolition. As a result of the local pressure the council agreed to try to retain the building, and to find someone prepared to lease and repair it. In 1983 a 125-year lease was agreed with the present lessees, Mr P. Lancashire (an architect) and Miss G. Harwood, who had already carried out similar schemes with redundant industrial buildings.

It was decided that the greater part of the building (most of the ground and first floors) should be converted into craft units, both for manufacture and for sale of goods, while the lofts and part of the first floor should become offices and studios, all available for letting. As far as the craft units were concerned, there eventually proved to be insufficient response to fill all these, so that some of them are now purely retail shops, including a small restaurant.

The northern section of the building was found to be in such a bad condition that its upper storey had to be taken down and rebuilt. This rebuilt section has walls of timber framing, weatherboarded externally, and a slate roof in place of the former corrugated iron. Considerable amounts of repair were needed to the rest of the building, and new windows and doors of an appropriately industrial character have been inserted along the main west frontage, which adjoins the car park. Roof lights have been inserted to

*Interior of the ground floor,
showing the old well.*

serve the offices in the lofts. The old brick factory chimney has been
kept, though no longer in use.

As with most industrial buildings of this type, there was a
considerable amount of exposed timber internally, in the form of
roof trusses, floor beams and supports. Some of these have had to be
covered to comply with the Building and Fire Regulations, but it
was possible to leave some exposed, by doubling up the beams and
by carrying out charring tests on the timber, proving its ability to
stand up to fire. An external spiral fire escape staircase has been built
at the north end of the building, in addition to the new internal
stairs. The internal replanning has been designed to retain the
character of the building as far as possible. On the ground floor an
old well has been kept, as have some surviving pieces of machinery.
Simple brick and timber finishes have been used throughout.
Externally, care has been taken to avoid garish signs which can
easily spoil a scheme of this kind. Two painted hanging signs over
the main entrances, and a movable standing sign set out when the
restaurant is open, are the only external indications of the use of the
building.

The scheme was privately funded by the lessees, without any
grants, and is proving financially viable. The total floor space is

Industrial buildings: case studies

12,000 square feet, and includes twenty craft units or shops. A rescue operation of this kind could probably only have been carried out by a private developer with the imagination to see the possibilities of an apparently unpromising building. While such work might have attracted some government grant under the Urban Development Grant Scheme, or from the Development Commission if it had been in an area of high unemployment, this would have been unlikely in an area such as Lewes. The building was not of sufficient historic or architectural interest to have attracted historic buildings grants, but there is no doubt that its rehabilitation has provided an attractive and well-used complex in a historic town. Mr Lancashire was responsible for the design.

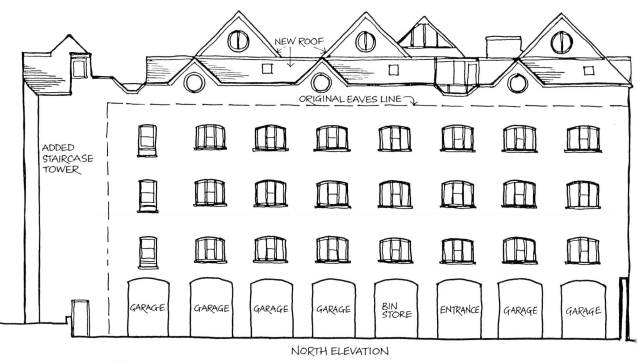

NORTH ELEVATION

THE MALTINGS · LONG ST. SHERBORNE

Interior before conversion, showing the cast iron columns supporting the vaulting.

The Maltings, Long Street, Sherborne, Dorset

This building, which is listed Grade II, is a prominent feature in the street. It was built *c.* 1820 as part of a brewery established in 1796, and in spite of its name was probably not originally a malt house. After its initial use ended, it became for a time a grain store, and was bought by the present owners, Messrs Hunt's Dairies (now Hunt's Frozen Foods) in 1978, after the previous owner had obtained planning permission for conversion to flats.

The building was four storeys high, and had walls of the local Sherborne stone. The original roof covering had been replaced by corrugated iron. The interior construction was of particular interest; the intermediate floors being of solid brick construction, forming a range of shallow barrel vaults carried on cast iron beams, the ends of which were locked round the tops of cast iron columns. At right angles to the main beams was a series of iron tie-rods, just above the level of the springing of the vaults. This form of construction was not unusual for nineteenth-century industrial buildings, but this is believed to be the only surviving example in southwest England. The cast iron beams and columns were probably made in Bristol or South Wales.

The original windows were segmental-headed and had cast iron frames with pivoted opening lights, a common industrial type. On the ground floor of the east front was a range of segmental-arched openings, probably originally cart sheds. At the rear were a number of lower outbuildings of similar construction, and similar, or later nineteenth-century date.

The architects for the scheme were first employed by the agents handling the sale, and were asked to produce plans illustrating the possibilities of the building for residential use. The original scheme was for twenty-six flats, but these were later reduced to twenty-four.

127

The east wall, before (LEFT) and after (BELOW) restoration, showing the new windows and the treatment of the arched openings on the ground floor.

It was the aim of the new owner to carry out the work in a manner sympathetic to the building, although it involved the demolition of all the rear out-buildings, and the insertion of a number of new windows, particularly on the north (road) frontage, and on the west, also visible from the road. As Sherborne stone is no longer quarried, a reconstructed stone, specially made to match the old stone as closely as possible, has been used for any necessary new walls, and for making good after demolition. It did not prove practicable to retain the old cast iron windows, and new, plain stained timber windows have been used throughout. The new window openings are segmental-headed to match those existing, but in the new openings the window frames have been recessed, with splayed jambs, to admit more light through the thick walls. In the existing openings, the frames have been set flush with the outer wall face, as before.

On the ground floor one of the large arched openings has been used to form a main entrance, another is a store, while the rest have become garages. The architects did not consider that any form of modern garage door would be appropriate, and iron gates have been fitted instead, maintaining the feeling of deep openings while providing some security.

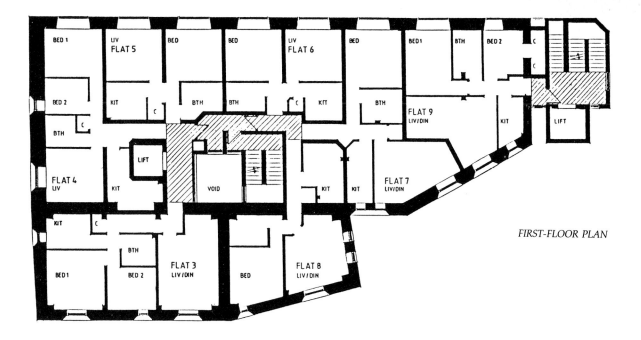

FIRST-FLOOR PLAN

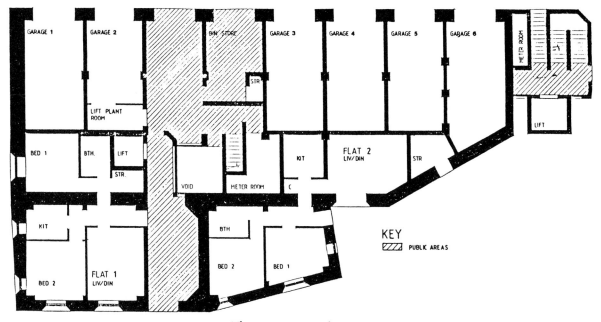

GROUND-FLOOR PLAN

The existing roof was in poor repair, and a new roof has been constructed, partly flat but incorporating a range of three pitched slated gabled roofs parallel to the street. This new roof is carried on timber columns, built off the old top floor, and supporting a flitched timber ring beam, which in turn supports the roof trusses. The weight of this new roof, being carried on the old vaulted floor, which in turn is now supported on the new party walls described below, has thus not placed any additional load on the old outer walls. The construction of this roof has, however, involved some

129

raising of the walls, and this has been done in matching natural stone. Four flats have been formed in the roof space, with sloping ceilings producing interesting room shapes, and fine views over the town and surrounding area. The rest of the building has been planned with two flats on the ground floor, seven on the first floor, six on the second floor, and five on the third floor. The flats vary in size, some having one, some two, and a few three bedrooms. As far as possible the new dividing walls coincide with the lines of the main beams, to maintain the vaulted ceilings in each room. In order to comply with the fire regulations and to avoid having to encase the cast iron columns, the floors are now supported on new solid party walls extending through the full height of the building. The columns, no longer considered to be load-bearing, are left exposed in the rooms, and the undersides of the vaults have been coated with a textured plaster.

At the south end of the building a new staircase tower has been built, giving access to one flat on the first floor, and providing a second access and escape to one flat on each of the second and third floors (these are the three-bedroomed flats), and to one in the roof space on the fourth floor. Access to the other flats is from a new internal staircase near the centre of the building. Since this produced a 'single staircase' situation as far as the fire regulations were concerned, special precautions were necessary to protect the stair shaft from smoke in case of fire. A full-height void, or light well, has been formed adjoining the stair well, with louvred vents in its walls, designed to draw air from the void into the stair well on the operation of the smoke detection system, creating a pressurised lobby. This will mean that the air pressure in the stair well will be higher than that in the flats, so that any smoke from a fire in a flat should be kept out of the stair well, enabling the occupants to escape. Each flat is fitted with smoke detectors and an alarm system. In the fourth-floor flats in the roof space, some of the rooms have timber boarded ceilings, and these have been treated with a fire-retarding intumescent paint.

The work was carried out by the owner on a direct labour basis. The architects were C.H. Design Partnership of Sherborne. It is proposed to add a new wing to the building, on the east, to provide more flats in due course. This scheme has secured the preservation of an interesting early industrial building. Its appearance has inevitably been altered to some extent by the construction of the new roof and insertion of new windows. It is perhaps unfortunate that some of the outbuildings could not have been saved, since a building of this type would not have existed in isolation, but as part of a complex. These changes were probably unavoidable once the decision had been made to convert the building to residential use, and no other use may have been viable in this case. A real effort has been made, though, to retain the rather severe industrial character, and some very pleasant flats have been created.

ABOVE LEFT *Interior of one of the top-floor rooms formed in the roof.* LEFT *A kitchen, showing the old vaulting.* ABOVE *The exterior of the new roof structure.*

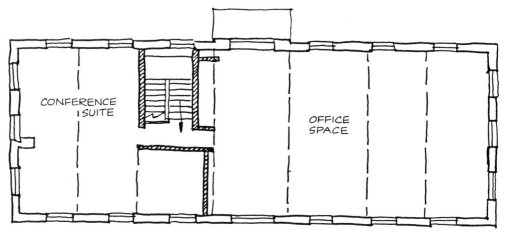

SECOND FLOOR

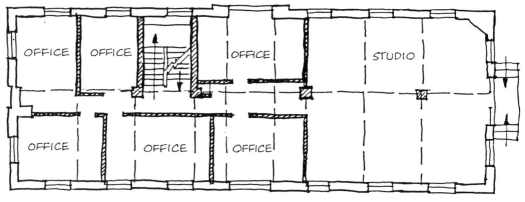

FIRST FLOOR

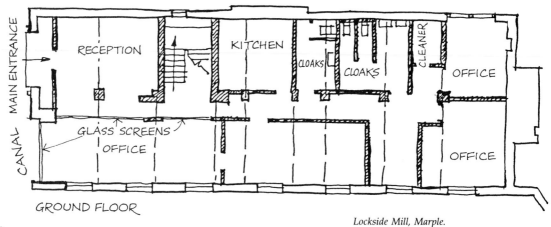

GROUND FLOOR

Lockside Mill, Marple.

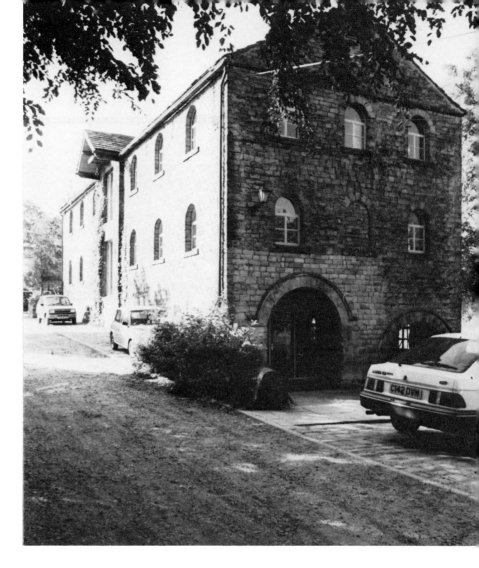

Lockside Mill, Saint Martin's Road, Marple, Cheshire

The restoration of many previously disused canals has often resulted in the restoration, and conversion to new uses, of canalside structures. Lockside Mill, at Marple, is an interesting example of this. It is situated on the Peak Forest Canal, near the top of the noted Marple flight of locks. The canal was completed in 1800, although the locks themselves were not in operation until a few years later, replacing a temporary tramway. Like many canals, the Peak Forest fell into disuse after the Second World War, but it has now been restored and re-opened, forming a popular cruising waterway and an attractive feature of the town.

Lockside Mill, a Grade II listed building, was reputedly built between 1795 and 1799. If this is so, it anticipated the construction of the locks, since it was clearly designed to allow for the direct

The new iron staircase, in keeping with the building.

entry of canal boats at its lowest level. In spite of its name it was probably a warehouse rather than a mill. It was built of stone, with a low-pitched stone slate roof. On the road front it was two storeys high, while the frontage to the canal was of three storeys, incorporating a basement with the original boat entry. On all floors there were ranges of round-arched windows, and on the top floor there were gabled lucarnes and sack hoists, facing both the canal and the road, with access doors below them.

After the canal ceased use for commercial traffic, the building had various uses as a workshop and store, and by 1975 it had become rather derelict. At this stage it was seen by Mr McFarland Davidson, an interior designer with a firm of architects, who felt that it could be converted for office use. He therefore negotiated a purchase with the owner, and applied for planning permission for change of use to offices. This was at first refused by the local authority, on the grounds that the area was primarily residential and that the only access was from an unmade road. An appeal against this refusal was, however, successful, and permission was granted subject to certain conditions. The approved use was for an architect's office, but as the firm did not require the whole building for themselves, any other tenancies have to be specifically approved by the local authority, to prevent any uses unsuitable for a residential area. At present (1986), apart from the architects, the building is used by an insurance agency, an office furnisher, a graphic designer and a computer software firm. The basement accommodates a general reception area, cloakrooms and kitchen serving all occupants, and one of the office suites, while the upper floors are used entirely as offices. The work was completed and the offices occupied from 1977 onwards.

The main structure was generally in sound condition, but much internal remodelling was necessary. The existing, quite interesting timber roof was retained, the trusses forming a feature of the top floor offices. A completely new staircase was constructed in metal, of open-tread form, a frankly industrial design quite suited to the building. Most of the new internal partitions are non-loadbearing, and have been modified to suit the various occupants. The existing windows have been retained and repaired, but the old upper floor access doors have been replaced with simple glazing.

Externally it was necessary to provide car parking space, and this has been combined with some attractive hard landscaping, appropriate to the building and also enhancing the setting of the canal. This section of the work was carried out as part of a Youth Training Scheme, under the Manpower Services Commission. The offices have proved popular. The setting is attractive and quiet, the land on the opposite side of the canal being laid out as a public park. At the same time there is easy access to Manchester by road or rail. The architects for the scheme were the Russell and Wheatcroft Design Partnership, and the present owners are the Lockside Partnership, architects, of which the original designer is now a member.

RIGHT *Interior, showing the original entrance for boats.* BELOW *Exterior from the canal.*

The Canal Centre, The Wharf, Devizes, Wiltshire

The Kennet and Avon Canal was one of the last to be constructed, the designer being Sir John Rennie. After a comparatively short time much of its trade was taken by the Great Western Railway, and at the end of the Second World War it was threatened with complete closure. This was opposed by a local society which eventually became the Kennet and Avon Canal Trust. As a result of this opposition, and the work of the Trust in raising funds for restoration, much of the canal is now open to navigation again, and it is hoped that the whole of the waterway will be in use by 1990.

As with many canal restoration schemes, this one has resulted in the repair and conversion of a number of canal buildings, and the work at Devizes Wharf is a good example of co-operation between official and voluntary bodies. In the heyday of the canal the wharf belonged to the (former) Borough of Devizes, who leased it to the Devizes Wharf Company. The two main buildings on the wharf were a brick warehouse, close by and parallel to the canal, and a long granary at right angles to the canal, this last being the more

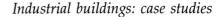

interesting structure. It was two-storeyed, with plastered walls, a low-pitched slate roof, and a two-storeyed open gallery, carried on timber posts, along one side.

After the construction of the railway, the wharf became less profitable and reverted to the Borough. Parts of it were still used for canal traffic, but other parts, including the granary, were now used for general storage, the granary becoming for a time a bonded warehouse. Eventually the Borough took over the whole wharf as a depot for its works department, the warehouse becoming a maintenance workshop, and the granary altered to accommodate dust carts, part of the gallery being removed and the floor levels altered.

At the re-organisation of local government in 1974, the wharf passed to the county council, who leased it back to the newly formed district council at a peppercorn rent. At this stage it could easily have been redeveloped and the original buildings lost, but by then the restoration of the canal was in hand and it was proposed to use the whole site for amenity purposes in connection with this. Fortunately the vacation of some local army barracks in 1978 meant that the council could relocate their works department depot, thus freeing the wharf buildings for other uses. The Canal Trust was asked to suggest uses for the buildings, in consultation with other local organisations. Plans were prepared to convert the granary into a meeting room, about five club rooms, a canal museum, offices for the Trust and for its local branch, and a combined canal shop and tourist information centre.

The exterior of the building has been restored to its original state, replacing the lost section of the gallery. The interior was remodelled as necessary to suit the new uses. By March 1980 the Trust office had been completed, and the tourist office was opened in the following May. The completion of the other rooms followed. Much of the internal work was done by Trust volunteers, the main structural work being done by the district council. The original idea for a local canal museum has been expanded, to include the interpretation of the whole canal. Grants for this part of the work were obtained from the Carnegie Trust, the Southern Tourist Board, and the Countryside Commission.

The brick warehouse is also used by the Trust as a meeting room and theatre, and the whole of the site has been landscaped by the district council. Siting the tourist information office here has helped to make visitors to the town more aware of the canal, and a once rather derelict area is being given a new lease of life.

8 Large houses

Threats to large houses, and concern for their preservation, have received considerable publicity over recent years, thanks partly to the activities of such organisations as Save Britain's Heritage. Social changes, taxation and inflation, particularly since the Second World War, have meant that many of these houses are no longer viable as single family homes. The problem has sometimes been exacerbated by the owners, perhaps needing money for essential repairs or to meet Estate Duty or its successor taxes, having sold off part of the surrounding land, thus reducing still further the income available for maintenance. As a result, often the only hope for the preservation of these large houses lies in their adaptation to new uses.

Another threat to the continuation of these houses as single residences occurs when they are on the edge of an expanding town, or affected by a major road proposal. The consequent damage to the environment, and loss of privacy, may make an owner decide to sell and move elsewhere. In these cases the whole site may be bought by the local authority, primarily to preserve the ground as an open space, the house itself sometimes being regarded as something of an embarrassment.

In a few cases the government has intervened to save a particularly fine house and prevent the dispersal of its contents, sometimes through the agency of the National Heritage Memorial Fund. All too often, though, if a large house comes on to the market the contents are sold off separately, to obtain the maximum return.

Before looking at possible new uses for these houses we must remember that they vary greatly, both in size and type. The term 'large house' can cover anything from palaces such as Blenheim and Castle Howard, to more modest manor and town houses. In design, too, we see many variations. First, there are the houses of medieval or Tudor origin, with a large open hall as their main feature, and ranges of smaller rooms, perhaps planned round a courtyard. Then we find houses which originated in this form, but were largely remodelled in the eighteenth century. Next, there are the eighteenth and nineteenth-century houses of formal, classical design, often symmetrical in plan, and, lastly, the nineteenth-century houses, perhaps based on medieval models, which reflect also the individual ideas of their owners and designers. All these differences will have to be taken into account when considering suitable alternative uses,

Argyle's Lodging, Stirling, Scotland. A fine town house now a youth hostel.

The Wardrobe, Salisbury, Wiltshire, in the Cathedral Close. A large house, probably of medieval origin, now houses a military museum with a Landmark Trust holiday flat in the roof space.

and it must be remembered that with houses of this type the interiors are often as important as the exteriors.

What, then, are the possible uses for these large houses?

First, there are those which, together with their contents and their gardens, are of such national importance that they should remain unaltered. This will mean preservation as a museum piece, probably open to the public, and perhaps with the owner or a curator occupying part of the building. Many fine houses are being preserved in this way, by their original owners, the Department of the Environment, or the Historic Buildings and Monuments Commission, by voluntary bodies such as the National Trust, and by local authorities. Although the house itself may be largely unaltered (this certainly being the objective), this does represent a major change of use from that of a private family house. It will be necessary to provide for efficient and safe circulation round the house for the public, possibly involving some minor internal replanning. The fire authority will require adequate means of escape, and a system of smoke detectors and sprinklers may have to be installed. Provision will also be needed for supervision of the public in the interests of security, perhaps by means of closed-circuit television or a burglar alarm system.

Arrangements will also have to be made for car parking, preferably where it will not affect the setting of the house, and, where appropriate, for suitable access for disabled people. Facilities such as cloakrooms, refreshment rooms and souvenir shops are also likely to be necessary, and all these things should be considered at the start of the project, to avoid makeshift alterations and additions. There is always the danger that the work needed to make such a use viable, providing adequate income for maintenance, may result in the loss of much of the original atmosphere of the house. A delicate balance has to be maintained between preservation and public enjoyment. This is exemplified by the way in which, in some National Trust houses, the natural and artificial lighting in some rooms has had to be reduced to avoid damage to valuable tapestries and other textiles.

For many large houses, though, this type of preservation is not possible. The contents may already have been dispersed, and the house itself not be of sufficient interest to attract enough visitors to produce an adequate income for maintenance. Some other solution has to be found.

The next alternative to be considered is the division of the house into a number of individual units, either as separate houses, flats or maisonettes. The practicality of such schemes will depend on the plan of the house itself; some will divide quite readily, without major alterations, while others will present more difficulties. Let us look at some of the problems which may arise.

First, if the house is to be divided *horizontally*, into flats, there are likely to be some difficulties with the Building and Fire Regulations. Standards, both of sound insulation and fire-resistance, required between flats are likely to be higher than those provided by the existing floors. Up-grading these can be expensive, and particularly difficult if there are ornamental ceilings and cornices, and specialist advice should be obtained. The regulations referring to means of escape can also present problems. Fortunately, these larger houses generally have two or more staircases, which can be used to provide alternative means of escape, but they may have to be up-graded in ways which can be damaging architecturally, particularly to the main staircase, which is often an important feature of the house. The walls surrounding the stairs will also have to be protected, which can be difficult if, as often, they are of timber stud construction and are panelled or have ornamental plasterwork on both sides. These problems can be overcome, but often only at considerable expense, which must be anticipated at the start of the scheme. Original panelled doors may not have an acceptable standard of fire-

A town house in Worcester, converted to flats by a housing association.

resistance, and may have to be modified or supplemented by additional doors in new lobbies within the rooms.

In many cases, *vertical* division into houses rather than flats causes fewer problems, particularly if existing solid cross-walls can be used as party walls. Here again, though, if the resultant houses are of more than two storeys the regulations can create problems, and an early discussion with the appropriate authorities is essential, so that these matters can be sorted out before any final plans are prepared. Quite apart from the problems of complying with these statutory requirements, it may be desired to divide up large rooms to produce a more workable plan. This will need great care, especially in rooms with good panelling, ceilings and other features. Where possible, solid divisions should be avoided, in favour of an open-plan type layout. It may be decided to instal some form of central heating, making the existing fireplaces redundant, but if these are contemporary with the house, or good later examples, they should not be removed. If they are sealed, care should be taken to provide ventilation to the flue, to avoid problems with condensation. The tendency to remove not only the fireplaces but complete chimney stacks, in order to obtain maximum floor space, is most undesirable. First, the external chimney stacks are often important features of the design, and should not be lost, and, equally important, removal of the stacks can cause structural problems. I am speaking only of the *original* stacks; it may sometimes be better to remove later inserted stacks, especially if, as sometimes happens, they are themselves damaging the structure.

Provision of the necessary additional plumbing and drainage will also need care. Too many fine houses, converted in this way, have been disfigured by unsightly pipework, due largely to lack of forethought. There is no need today for soil and waste pipes to be fixed on external walls. From all points of view (except perhaps immediate cheapness!) they are better placed internally, in ducts, and the houses or flats planned in such a way as to avoid spoiling important rooms. The fact that bathrooms can be artificially lit and ventilated may avoid the need to insert additional windows, which generally proclaim their purpose all too obviously. The installation of central heating will also need care, to avoid unsightly pipe runs and inappropriately sited radiators.

As well as the house itself, the gardens and grounds will have to be considered. In some cases it may be possible to divide these, particularly if the house itself has been divided vertically, but often it will be best to arrange for some communal or overall scheme of maintenance. This should include not only the lawns, flower beds and paths, but also any terraces, ha-has, gazebos, follies or other garden buildings, all of which contribute to the setting of the house, and which are likely to deteriorate unless definite arrangements are made for the responsibility for their maintenance. In this connection, it is generally best for the whole house to remain in one ownership,

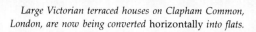

Large Victorian terraced houses on Clapham Common, London, are now being converted horizontally *into flats.*

A town house in Dorchester, Dorset, believed to have been chosen by Thomas Hardy as the home of 'The Mayor of Casterbridge'. It is now a bank. The fine facade has been preserved, but commercial conversion has destroyed much of the interior.

the houses or flats being leased rather than sold freehold, and with a management agreement to secure an overall standard of maintenance. If this is not done and one or more of the units are neglected, the whole house will eventually deteriorate.

In spite of the problems outlined above, a sensitive residential conversion is often the best way of preserving a large house, since it is in a sense a continuation of the original use. The developer must, though, resist the temptation to cram in the maximum number of units, regardless of the effect on the character of the house.

Another possible use for these larger houses is as an office building, either for one firm or a public authority using the whole house, or by dividing it into a number of separate units. The viability of such a use, and the likelihood of its obtaining planning permission, will depend much on its siting and the overall land use policy for the area.

Many of the problems arising from this use will be similar to those discussed in connection with residential conversion, but there will be some differences. The requirements for sound insulation between the different storeys may well be less stringent for office use, but those for fire resistance and means of escape will still apply.

Restrictions may be placed on the use of parts of the building, particularly the top floor. In addition, it is likely that the required floor loading figures for offices will be higher than those for flats or houses, involving some strengthening of existing floors.

As with residential conversions, there may well be pressure to divide up large rooms, and when the usual standard office partitions are used the effect on a fine room can be most unfortunate. The standards of artificial lighting required in offices, and the need for economy in running costs also often means that fluorescent lighting is installed, looking completely out of character in a period room. It is clearly best if the larger, finer rooms of the house can be left unaltered, being used for, say, board rooms and conference rooms, and for a fine entrance to be kept clear as a reception area.

Provision will probably have to be made for car parking, and all too often this is sited immediately in front of the house, perhaps involving the destruction of part of the garden. There may also be a desire for advertising and other signs, and these will need to be treated with great care. Perhaps the most serious problem, though, will arise simply because the new use proves too successful, and outgrows the original building, resulting in pressure for additional accommodation. This may be provided by extending the house—a subject we shall look at later in this chapter—but all too often we see a fine house, converted into offices and surrounded by prefabricated structures, sometimes described as 'temporary' but often proving all too permanent. This, I am afraid, is particularly common in houses taken over as offices by public authorities. The highway authority may require an improved access to accommodate the anticipated increase in traffic, and this will need careful treatment. Original fine entrance gateways should not be destroyed or damaged.

Office use, then, can be successful, but only if the limitations of the building are accepted, and adequate financial provision made for the proper maintenance of the house and its surroundings. Use by one firm is generally preferable, but if the house is to be divided and let to different occupants there should be a firm maintenance arrangement, to ensure that the whole building is kept in a good state of repair.

Another use for the larger house is for some kind of institutional purpose. This can include schools, colleges, conference centres, hospitals and nursing homes, and residential homes for the elderly or disabled. As with office use, the likelihood of obtaining planning consent will depend on the location of the house, as well as the possible effect on its character. The problems likely to arise from such uses are again similar to those we have considered in relation to residential and office use. Indeed, for such uses as hospitals, nursing and residential homes the fire precautions requirements are likely to be even more stringent and perhaps impossible to comply with, without drastic alterations to the house. This must be

Rothley Court, near Loughborough. A large country house, now an hotel.

anticipated before considering such a use for a house of any quality. One particular problem is that the fire precautions requirements are periodically altered and strengthened. Initial approval may be obtained for a scheme, and all the required works carried out. It is then possible that a few years later the authority will carry out another inspection, and require further works. In this connection, if external fire escape staircases are planned or have been constructed, under the present Building Regulations these often have to be enclosed, and it can be very difficult to incorporate these without disfiguring the exterior of the house.

It is generally best for the more important rooms in the house to be kept for public or communal use, certainly not for sleeping accommodation, where the requirements are particularly strict. The installation of lifts, probably more necessary for these uses than for most others, will also need careful treatment to avoid spoiling, for instance, a fine staircase or entrance hall. Just as we have seen with office conversions, there may be the problem of the use outgrowing the building, with the resultant crop of prefabs surrounding the house. It is not always possible to foresee the eventual development of any scheme, but it should be sufficiently well funded to ensure the proper maintenance of the house, and the quality of any future additions.

A number of large houses have been converted to hotels and guest houses, sometimes incorporating a restaurant open to the general public. Here again, planning consent will depend largely on the siting of the house. Country house hotels, in attractive and quiet surroundings, are understandably popular. Problems arising under the Building and Fire Regulations are likely to be similar to those already discussed, and if the premises are to be licensed the licensing authority will impose its own standards, which may differ from those of the building control and fire authorities. Early discussion with all parties is essential. There is one other problem likely to arise with a hotel conversion: it is usual nowadays to provide all bedrooms with private bathrooms, and this may involve dividing up rooms with good cornices and other features. The resultant plumbing, too, will need to be carefully designed, avoiding visible pipework. Often the best and larger rooms can be kept for public or communal purposes, avoiding the need for alterations. The open hall of a medieval or Tudor house makes a splendid dining room, reminiscent of the Oxford and Cambridge colleges. Many large houses have underground, or semi-underground, cellars, sometimes with vaulted ceilings. These have been successfully converted into restaurants and bars, but independent external access is generally necessary to comply with the fire regulations.

For all these uses, we have considered the case of the use outgrowing the building, and the all-too-frequent solution of the problem by putting up so-called 'temporary' buildings. There may, however, be a desire to extend the house itself, and here the question of design is all-important. Should the new work copy the

ABOVE *The medieval chapel attached to Rothley Court.* BELOW LEFT *The stables at Rothley Court, converted to hotel accommodation.*

A fine Georgian house in Salisbury has been converted to offices. This use has necessitated the building of a large rear wing, which has been done successfully in a frankly modern style (RIGHT) . The street frontage is unchanged.

old, or should it be a frankly modern addition, as was generally the case in the past? I do not think that we can be too dogmatic about this—every house is different and there is no universal solution to the problem. It is most important to appoint an architect who has a genuine appreciation of the building, and who is not concerned primarily with leaving his mark on it! With a formal, symmetrical house in classical style it will be difficult to design a suitable extension, and any attempt to reproduce the original style will risk devaluing the house itself. Sometimes the answer will be to extend in a very simple, traditional style, such as might have been used for the original servants' quarters, keeping the new work subservient to the old. With a less formally designed house, perhaps one of medieval origin which has already been enlarged and altered, the problem may be rather easier, as there is less risk of destroying a symmetrical composition. If such a house already has work of more than one period there could be a case for an extension of

unmistakably twentieth-century date, but it will need to be carried out with great care and sensitivity—a bad modern design will probably look worse than a bad or mediocre traditional one.

At the start of this chapter I pointed out that many of these large houses had been altered in the past; a medieval hall may have been remodelled in the eighteenth century. It is therefore possible that, during the course of the conversion work, evidence of the original form of the house may be uncovered. This should not be destroyed, or even covered up again without proper investigation, and specialist advice should be obtained. It may not always be possible, or desirable, to leave early work exposed, although this can sometimes add interest to the house, but it should certainly be fully recorded.

I have also drawn attention to the need for most of these new uses to comply with the Building and Fire Regulations, and the fact that this can sometimes affect the character of the house. It must be

emphasised that, in the case of a listed building, any such works will
need listed building consent, and it will be appreciated that there
could be a conflict of interests here. For this reason I have stressed
the need for early consultations with *all* the relevant authorities, as
it may sometimes be possible to work out an acceptable compromise solution which may involve applying for a relaxation of the
Building Regulations. If work is carried out without listed building
consent it will be no defence to show that it was required under
other legislation!

Before leaving the subject of the large house, I should like to raise
the question of what is sometimes called 'enabling development'.
The owner, or a prospective purchaser, may maintain that he can
only afford to restore the house in an appropriate manner if he is
given permission to develop part of the grounds—generally for
housing, which can then help to finance the scheme. This is a
persuasive argument, but all too often planning permission has been
given, only for the authority to find that the new development is
carried out and the original house still left to decay. Eventually there
may be pressure to allow demolition as the house is now 'beyond
repair'. Indeed, once the setting of a good house has been largely
destroyed by allowing such development and the loss of much of
the grounds, it often becomes increasingly difficult to find a suitable
use, or to attract a new purchaser prepared to meet the cost of
repairs. There may be some cases where a certain amount of such
development is justified, but it will need to be looked at very
carefully by the planning authority. Sometimes it will be appropriate to make any approval subject to a condition requiring the house
to be put into repair before any new development is started.

Pyt House, Newtown, near Tisbury, Wiltshire

The core of Pyt House, a Grade I listed building, is an eighteenth-century house which replaced an earlier, probably sixteenth-century, building. It was built for the Bennett family, who had owned the land since the thirteenth century, except for a short period after the Civil War in the seventeenth century. The eighteenth-century house was of ashlar stone, roughly square in plan; it was greatly enlarged and remodelled *c.* 1805, transforming it into a two-storeyed Palladian villa of H-shaped plan, but with full-height colonnaded porticos filling the recesses in each of the side elevations. On the entrance front was a projecting pedimented portico, supported on four Ionic columns. The walls were of ashlar stone, and the low-pitched roofs of slate, behind a moulded parapet. The house had sash windows, with tripartite windows in shallow segmental-headed recesses on the ground floor of the side elevations, flanking the recessed sections. Internally, one of the main features was the principal staircase, in the centre of the house. This consisted of a free-standing flight in the centre of the hall, leading up to a half landing on two levels, marked by Ionic columns, these different levels reflecting differences in ground-floor ceiling heights of the original and later sections of the house. From this landing two returned flights of stairs led up to the first floor. The architect for this work is not known; the design shows some affinity with that of the nearby Philipps House, by Sir Jeffrey Wyattville, but Pyt House may have been designed by the then owner, John Bennett, himself an amateur architect.

In 1891 the house was again enlarged, this time by the addition

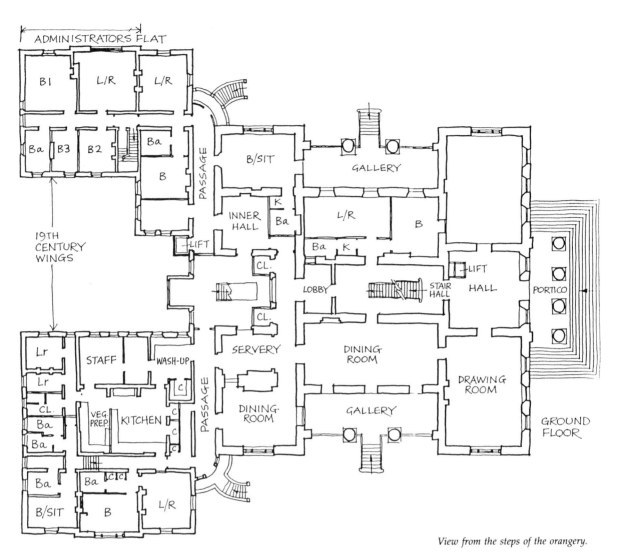

ADMINISTRATORS FLAT

B1   L/R   L/R

Ba   B3   B2   Ba

B

19TH
CENTURY
WINGS

PASSAGE

LIFT

B/SIT

INNER
HALL

K

Ba

CL.

CL.

GALLERY

L/R   B

Ba   K

LOBBY   STAIR
HALL

LIFT

HALL

PORTICO

Lr

Lr

CL.

Ba

Ba

Ba

B/SIT

STAFF   WASH-UP

VEG.
PREP.   KITCHEN

c

c

c

c

Ba   C C

B   L/R

PASSAGE

SERVERY

DINING
ROOM

DINING
ROOM

GALLERY

DRAWING
ROOM

GROUND
FLOOR

View from the steps of the orangery.

152

The entrance front.

of two service wings at the rear, matching the general style of the rest of the house. At the same time, rather unfortunately, the glazing bars were removed from many of the sash windows. The house remained in the ownership of the Bennett family until the late 1940s. During the Second World War it was for a time occupied by the army, and after the war it was inherited by a distant relative, Sir Arthur Rumbold. By this time the house was in a very dilapidated

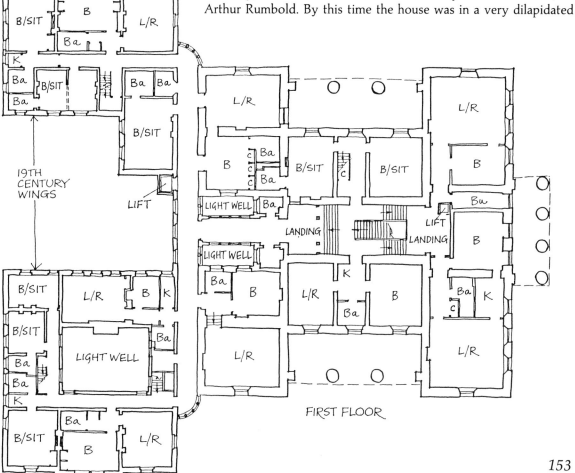

FIRST FLOOR

LEFT *and* RIGHT *The main staircase and upper landing.*

BELOW *One of the flat kitchenettes, concealed in a cupboard.*

condition, and in 1958 it was bought, with about six acres of land, by the Mutual Households Association.

This association had been founded in 1955 as a charity, also registered as a housing association under the *Industrial and Provident Societies Act*. Its purpose was two-fold. First, to preserve houses of historic importance, and second, to adapt them as apartments for letting as residential accommodation. In practice the association (now renamed the Country Houses Association Ltd) normally only acquires Grade I listed buildings, and the flats are let out to retired professional and similar people. The aim is always to carry out the necessary alterations in such a way as to retain the character of the houses, and great care is taken over such matters as dividing up large rooms to make more convenient units, and the installation of plumbing and other services. Although the flats are self-contained, the residents have all their meals in the communal dining room, and the flats themselves are only fitted with small kitchenettes, with a sink and points for a kettle, toaster, refrigerator, etc.

Pyt House was converted into twenty-seven flats, accommodating thirty-eight residents, and a flat for the administrators, a married

couple. The flats vary in size, some having a single bed-sitting room, and some a living room and separate bedroom. All flats have bathrooms and the whole house is centrally heated. In the main house, most of the principal ground-floor rooms are used for communal purposes, comprising the main entrance hall in which a lift has been installed, drawing room, morning room and two dining rooms. This has meant that these fine rooms have remained unaltered, and they have been appropriately furnished. Several

BELOW *One of the main ground-floor rooms.*

Large houses: case studies

Bennett family portraits have been left in the house, on loan from the vendor's family.

The original plan of the house has lent itself well to a conversion of this type, with few structural alterations being required. As there were already several staircases, with separate ones serving the two rear wings, there were no serious problems over fire precautions. As with other properties owned by the association, the grounds are communally maintained, and the general appearance is still that of a private house rather than a hotel or an institution. The orangery in the garden, a relic of the early eighteenth-century house, has been repaired for the use of the residents as a garden room.

Perhaps the only unfortunate feature, as far as the setting of the house is concerned, is that residents' cars are parked in the drive immediately in front of the main entrance. Although this is undoubtedly convenient, it does rather detract from the private domestic character of the building. The restoration of the glazing bars to the sash windows would be another, rather more expensive, improvement. This is, though, a good solution to the problem of the large country house, providing a suitable use and a high standard of maintenance with minimum alterations. The fact that the association is a non profit-making body probably means that there is less pressure to fit in as many units as possible, as one sometimes sees happen, to the detriment of the house, in a purely commercial venture of this type.

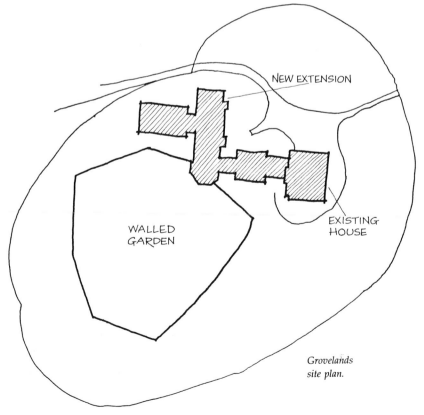

NEW EXTENSION

WALLED
GARDEN

EXISTING
HOUSE

*Grovelands
site plan.*

Grovelands, Southgate, London

The story of this house illustrates a number of the problems of the large country house which has been overtaken by urban expansion. The house, designed by John Nash in 1797 as a rural villa, was built for Walter Gray. It was of a compact rectangular plan form, with slightly projecting bays at each end of the front and rear elevations. On the front elevation the recess between these projections was filled with a slightly projecting Ionic portico, and there were similar porticos in the centres of the side elevations. The house was of two storeys, with cellars and attic, and had plastered walls with stone dressings, the capitals to the columns being made of a patent composition. The low-pitched roofs were slated, partly concealed behind parapets. On each side of the main front portico, on the ground floor, was a large tripartite sash window, with a recessed tympanum. Other windows were simple sashes, with glazing bars, and the attic had shallow oval windows. The best interior features

157

were the open staircase in the rear hall, and the room to the right of the main entrance, which had a vaulted ceiling and was painted to imitate a birdcage. The house stood in extensive grounds, landscaped by Repton.

After the death of the original owner the estate was bought by Mr J.D. Taylor, of the Taylor Walker Brewery, and on the death of his son in 1902 much of it was sold. The Southgate Urban District Council bought most of the land for a public park, and in 1916 the house became a military hospital. After 1948 it passed to the National Health Service, and continued in use as a hospital until 1976. Fortunately, the house survived largely unspoilt, although latterly only the ground floor was being used, because of problems with the fire regulations. After the closure, the house began to deteriorate and it was offered for sale, with sixteen acres of land, by the health authority. Various prospective purchasers showed interest, but no sale was concluded and the deterioration increased. By 1983 the council (now the London Borough of Enfield) were very concerned about Grovelands, but were unable even to consider serving a repairs notice as the house, being Crown property, was immune from compulsory purchase proceedings. Fortunately, at this stage the house and remaining grounds were bought by Community Psychiatric Centers, a private health care organisation who, in 1985, obtained planning permission for its conversion to a

LEFT *The 'birdcage' room, and* ABOVE *the main staircase.*

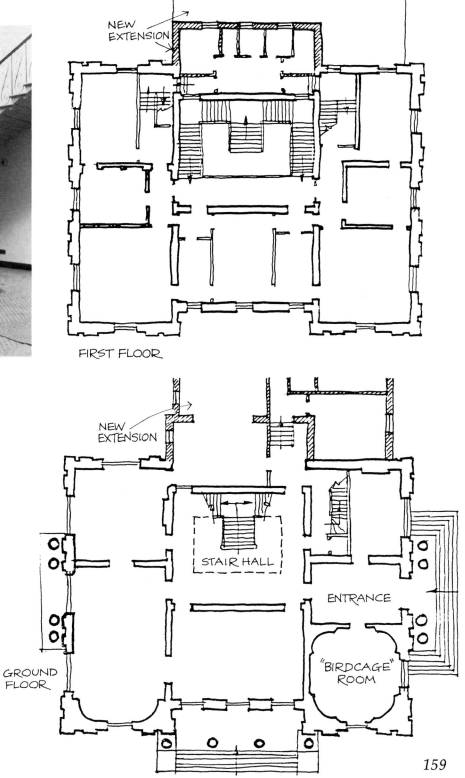

NEW
EXTENSION

FIRST FLOOR

NEW
EXTENSION

STAIR HALL

ENTRANCE

GROUND
FLOOR

"BIRDCAGE"
ROOM

159

Large houses: case studies

private psychiatric hospital. This permission was not obtained easily, since the new owners wanted to build a substantial new wing, more than doubling the size of the house, in order to make the scheme viable. As the house was a Grade I listed building the Department of the Environment had to give the final approval, and the Royal Fine Arts Commission were also consulted. The problem of designing an extension of this size was eventually solved by building out at the rear of the house, partly on the site of the old kitchen and outbuildings. Most of the new block, roughly T-shaped in plan, is of two storeys, but this is linked to the original house by a single-storey block. The new section is built in a neutral coloured brick, with low-pitched slate roofs, and its style, although traditional, has been kept simple to avoid competing with the original house. Use has been made of existing trees to help screen the new block and to prevent it from dominating the house.

All the accommodation for patients is contained in the new building, and this has simplified compliance with the Building and Fire Regulations. In the original house the ground-floor rooms are used as reception areas and for meetings; the first floor comprises consulting and waiting rooms, while the second floor is used mainly for medical records. These uses have avoided many of the problems which would have arisen had the house itself been used for patients. One new staircase has had to be inserted, from the first to the second floor, and two open archways on the first-floor landing have had to be infilled with fire-resisting screens and doors. There were very full consultations with the fire authority, and a waiver of regulations was obtained to avoid altering the original panelled doors. Smoke detectors have been installed throughout the building.

Very extensive repairs were needed to the house, as it had become badly affected by dry rot. All the internal plaster, which had been battened out from the walls, has had to be renewed, and great

ABOVE *Work on construction of the new wing, and* LEFT *the new extension, from the drive.* RIGHT *New fire doors inserted in arches in the first-floor landing.*

care has been taken to reinstate all the original ornamental work. The opportunity was taken to remove a number of later inserted partitions, restoring the original proportions of the main rooms. The roofs had to be completely reslated, with substantial renewal of the timbers. Most of the original outbuildings have been demolished, but one old stable block is to be converted to an occupational therapy unit. In the grounds, provision has had to be made for car parking, but the existing trees have been retained as far as possible, and it is proposed to restore the old walled garden, the walls of which retain an interesting hypocaust heating system, with ducts incorporated in the walling.

The hospital contains sixty-five beds, all in the new extension, and was opened in 1986. The cost of the work was just over £2,000,000, partly accounted for by the high cost of the repairs. No grants were obtained for the work. The architects were Bodnitz Allan and Partners, with Donald Insall and Associates as consultants. Permission is rarely granted for such a large extension to a Grade I house. In this case it seems to have been justified, since the house, which was in danger of demolition, has been restored to a very high standard. In less sensitive hands the result could have been very different, and this case is unlikely to set a precedent.

The old prison at Lincoln, now the local Record Office.

9 Schools and institutional buildings

Under this heading we shall be looking at small country schools, often with attached school houses, larger town schools of similar basic plan, the multi-storeyed grammar and board schools found in many towns, older grammar and charity schools, almshouses, orphanages and asylums in both urban and rural settings, and early workhouses.

Many of these institutions have closed in recent years, due largely to a fall in the school-age population, and the trend to replace large institutions with small family homes. Most of the old workhouses have been replaced by other forms of care. Although some of the buildings have been demolished, they were often substantially constructed, and sometimes of quite pleasant design, making them suitable for conversion for a variety of uses.

Starting with the small rural schools, generally of nineteenth-century date, these are often in a Gothic or Tudor style, and they have been popular subjects for residential conversion. On the other hand, there has sometimes been opposition to the closure of a village school, and even when this is unsuccessful in saving the school there may be a strong local feeling that the building should remain in community use, as a village hall, youth centre or even a small rural museum. Villagers, perhaps remembering that the school had originally been built by local public subscription, or as the gift to the parish from a former landowner, not unnaturally feel rather resentful when they discover that if they wish to retain the building for some community purpose they then have to raise the necessary funds to 'buy' it back from the Church, or the local authority, at residential market value. Where such feelings exist there may well be resistance to the idea of converting the school into a private house, and any intending purchaser should be aware of this.

Whatever new use is chosen, the building should be carefully inspected, as it will often be found that the original school has been enlarged. These later additions may not be in a sympathetic style, particularly the work of the immediate post-war years, and it is often best to remove these, together with the prefabricated class-rooms put up in the playground. If a residential use is approved, any alterations should respect the character of the original building. Most of these little schools consisted of a single large classroom or hall, open to the roof, and perhaps divided by a sliding-folding

A former village Temperance Hall in Dorset, converted to a house. The building has been preserved, but the dormers are rather unfortunate.

partition. There may be one or two smaller rooms, and perhaps an attached or adjoining school house. The house may be sold with the school, but all too often the authority will try to obtain separate planning permission for the school, so that the two buildings can be sold separately, at a higher price. It is clearly an advantage if the house and the school are kept in one ownership, as this will enable the smaller rooms to be planned within the house, leaving the large schoolroom open to the roof, thus retaining its proportions, avoiding altering the windows (sometimes found necessary when an intermediate floor is inserted), and enabling the often attractive open roof to be revealed. If it is essential to insert a floor in the hall, this is best treated as an open gallery, an approach similar to the one I have suggested for large barns. New dormers should be avoided if possible. If they have to be used, to provide adequate lighting at the upper level they should be kept small in scale, and in character with the style of the building.

As previously stated, these small schools are often very suitable for use as village halls, youth centres, day centres, club rooms and other community purposes. They can also be converted quite successfully as craft workshops, or shops, perhaps combined with a small museum, exhibition or information centre. The playground will normally provide adequate car parking space.

In towns, and in some larger villages, a larger version of the same basic school type is found. These schools often have a large

RIGHT, ABOVE *and* BELOW *An old school in Lincoln, converted to an hotel. The general external appearance has been retained.*

assembly hall, open to the roof, and perhaps divided by sliding-folding partitions. There are likely to be more smaller classrooms, sometimes planned on two floors, and possibly a school house. As with the smaller rural schools, there are likely to have been various additions, generally in rather a utilitarian style, and it may be possible to remove these. Schools of this type can often be converted for community use, for craft or light industry, again perhaps combined with a museum or exhibition space, or for shops. Some may be suitable for a youth hostel, or a residential study centre. When we come to consider residential use, these schools will probably be too large for conversion to a single house. Division into two or three houses, or into flats, may be feasible, depending on the design of the building. As with the rural schools, the playground area will probably provide adequate parking space for most uses—always supposing that it has not been sold separately with planning permission for development.

The substantial nature of most of these buildings means that they are not likely to present too many problems under the Building and Fire Regulations, although if the building is converted into flats the upper floors, if of timber, may have to be up-graded and their sound insulation improved. It will be an advantage if the large hall can be left open, but if it is necessary to divide it the original windows should be left unaltered, and great care taken with the designing of any dormers or roof lights.

165

Schools and institutional buildings

One problem often found with school conversion is that the window cill heights are likely to be quite high above the floor level, presumably to encourage the children to concentrate on their lessons rather than looking out of the windows! Sometimes it is possible to lower the cills without spoiling the general proportions, but, alternatively, advantage may be taken of the often high-ceilinged rooms to insert false floors at a higher level. As with other residential conversions the plumbing and other services should be carefully designed to avoid unsightly pipework, and the insertion of false floors may help in this. Apart from the main hall, which may have an interesting roof, these schools are unlikely to have many significant internal features.

We come next to the more typical urban school, of two or three storeys and fairly compact plan, such as were put up by the school boards and local authorities in the later nineteenth century. These are sometimes Gothic in design but the 'Queen Anne' style was also popular, particularly with the London County Council. In these schools the assembly hall is not so prominent an external feature as it is in the school types we have just considered. Although some form of community use is often appropriate, buildings of this type may convert more readily into flats, offices, hostels or hotels. They were generally substantially built, with fire-resisting floors and staircases, presenting few problems with the Building and Fire Regulations, except perhaps for the need to improve sound insulation and, possibly, to incorporate additional staircases. As with other schools the window cill levels may be rather high, but as the rooms themselves are probably higher than is required this problem is again best overcome by inserting false floors, which can also help to improve the sound insulation.

Although the main hall may not be a feature of the exterior, it may well have a good interior, extending through two storeys, and if possible it should remain open. It may be possible to exclude the hall from the flats or offices, and keep it as a hall available for letting for meetings or exhibitions. In a hotel or hostel the hall could be used as a dining room, or for some similar communal purpose. As we have seen with other buildings, if a school like this is converted into flats or offices there should be an overall management scheme to ensure that the whole building is maintained to an acceptable standard. This should include the immediate surroundings, as well as the actual building. For many uses it may be desirable to improve the setting provided by the old playground, by better paving and some planting.

A rather different approach may be called for in the case of the early grammar and charity schools, generally found in old towns but occasionally in a village. These can be of sixteenth, seventeenth or eighteenth-century date and are often of considerable architectural and historic interest. They may become redundant either because the school has outgrown its site and moved elsewhere, or because it

ABOVE *The old Grammar School, Faversham, Kent, converted as a Masonic Hall.*

At Chard in Somerset the old Grammar School is now a private house.

A former orphanage in process of conversion to new uses: The Royal Patriotic School (for full description see pp. 188-93).

has been closed or amalgamated with other schools in a scheme of educational reorganisation. In the past these buildings have sometimes been demolished in order to obtain the maximum price for the site, but this is now less likely to happen with buildings of real interest. It is important to find a new use which will preserve not only the exterior, but in many cases the interior, as this may be of equal interest. Like most other schools they will probably have been altered and extended over the centuries, and a careful historical survey should be carried out to ensure that the original structure and all features of interest are preserved. Generally some form of community use will be more appropriate than a residential conversion. If the latter is chosen, the planning of the house may have to be adapted to avoid destroying the character of the building. In particular, a fine hall, chapel or schoolroom should remain intact.

The next class of institutional building that may become available for conversion includes the nineteenth-century orphanages and asylums, sometimes found in towns but often in rural areas, perhaps reflecting the Victorian belief in the value of fresh air and, possibly, isolation from the rest of the community! These buildings are often in a Gothic style, planned on rather monastic lines, with ranges of two or three-storeyed buildings grouped round a courtyard, a large assembly hall, and sometimes a prominent gatehouse or entrance porch. In many cases the architectural pretensions of the exterior contrast with a rather stark interior.

Again, being substantially built, these buildings may convert quite readily into flats, offices and workshops, educational or conference centres, or hotels. As we have seen with other schools, there may be problems with high ceilings and cill levels, but again these can be overcome by the use of false floors. Apart perhaps from the main hall and chapel, the interiors are unlikely to contain many features of interest, and may well need some humanising. These buildings are often set in spacious grounds, and there may be a desire to develop these, generally with houses, in order to make the scheme more profitable. The possibility of permission being given will depend on the general planning policy for the area; there is likely to be opposition to the creation of a 'new town' in the open countryside. If any new development is to take place the setting of the original building should be preserved, leaving an adequate area round it.

Almshouses form another group of institutional buildings, and are found both in towns and in villages. Originally built to provide accommodation for poorer elderly people, they have sometimes in recent years been replaced by more convenient, or more pleasantly sited, new homes. This is particularly true of almshouses in towns, where the general environment may have deteriorated because of increased traffic or a change in the character of the area from residential to commercial.

The oldest, medieval type of almshouse was planned rather like a

A former almshouse at Ilford, now the headquarters of Interface (see Moulsham Mill, p. 109). Part of the chapel remains in use, but part has been taken for offices (LEFT).

simple church, the 'nave' being used for the living accommodation and the 'chancel' as a chapel. After the Reformation these alms-houses or hospices were generally replaced by ranges of small individual dwellings, sometimes with a central dining hall, and a chapel. The dwellings themselves were often very small, and where almshouses have remained in use they have often been replanned, combining two dwellings into one larger one.

Redundant almshouses have been converted for a number of uses. Residential conversion, into one or more normal sized houses, can be quite successful, and others have been made into offices, shops, community buildings and museums. Where possible the chapel should remain unaltered, especially if it retains its original furnishings. Two-storeyed almshouses may be converted horizontally, into flats or offices. As we have seen in other cases this may involve improving the fire-resistance and sound insulation of the floors. In some conversion schemes a number of the external doors may become redundant. These should if possible be retained, even if they have to be built up internally, to maintain the rhythm of the external

Napper's Mite, Dorchester, Dorset. These almshouses have been converted to shops, offices and a restaurant. The central arches lead into an attractive small courtyard.

A large block of almshouses on the outskirts of Gloucester has become a wine warehouse.

elevations. Also, in many almshouses, the chimney stacks form an important element in the design. Some or all of the fireplaces may no longer be required, but they should not be removed. Apart from spoiling the skyline, wholesale removal of chimneys, internally, may affect the stability of the structure. If it becomes necessary to combine the existing, often very small, rooms into larger ones this should be done, wherever possible, by removing non-loadbearing partitions. Almshouse windows may be rather small, with stone or heavy timber mullions, and leaded or cast iron lights. These should be retained, as enlarging the openings or even filling them with plain glass can destroy the small, intimate scale of these buildings.

Finally we have the early nineteenth-century workhouses, erected after the passing of the 1834 *Poor Law*, to replace the old parish poorhouses, and generally serving a group or 'Union' of parishes. Most of these were built to one of a small number of standard plans, often cruciform or Y-shaped, with wings radiating from a central space. Unlike the orphanages which generally favoured an ecclesiastical Gothic, the workhouses were generally in

a rather severe classical style, and although they were solidly built they showed a great economy of ornament, as well as of internal comfort! Some of them have been adapted as hospitals, or old people's homes, by the local authorities, but the stigma of the workhouse has often remained and it may be better to find a completely new use. Some have been converted into flats, and they could be equally suitable for offices, perhaps combined with workshops, or as residential or conference centres. As with most of the other institutional buildings they were generally of substantial construction, with fire-resisting floors and staircases, the main problems probably being with high ceilings and high window cill levels. In any conversion scheme the interiors will probably need some humanising, but the rather austere exteriors are best retained, their appearance being softened by attractive planting and landscaping rather than by dressing up the buildings with bow windows, 'bull's eyes' and pseudo-Spanish ironwork. Later additions, often of a so-called 'temporary' nature, which often obscure the original form of the building by filling parts of the space between the radiating wings, are generally best removed.

BELOW and LEFT *The Red Barracks, Weymouth, Dorset. These former cavalry barracks, dating from the Napoleonic Wars, were at one time threatened with demolition, but are being converted to flats, combined with some new housing in part of the former barrack square. They command fine views over the harbour.*

Saint Peter's Court, Mountsorrel, near Loughborough, Leicestershire

This was a fairly typical nineteenth-century church school, built in 1871, with walls of the local granite and roof of Swithland slate. The whole building was single-storeyed, with high rooms open to the roof. In plan it was roughly U-shaped. A range along the road frontage contained two classrooms, with a small connecting room. A range at right angles to this, running back from the road, contained the main hall, with a folding partition dividing this into two classrooms when required, while a wing at the rear of this, parallel to the road, contained a further large room. In the space between the two parallel wings were some lower outbuildings.

The school was built in a simple Gothic revival style with pairs of pointed-arched windows in the main ranges, and open timber roofs internally. As was usual with school buildings of this period, some of the window cill levels were rather high.

The school closed in 1981 and stood empty for a time. In 1982 it was bought by the East Midlands Housing Association for conversion into flats. In order to make the scheme viable it was necessary to insert intermediate first floors throughout the building. The positions of these floors were largely dictated by the levels of the ground-floor window heads, as it was considered important to retain the existing external appearance as far as possible. This would have made the ground-floor ceilings very high, and false ceilings have therefore been inserted, sloping upwards towards the outer

174

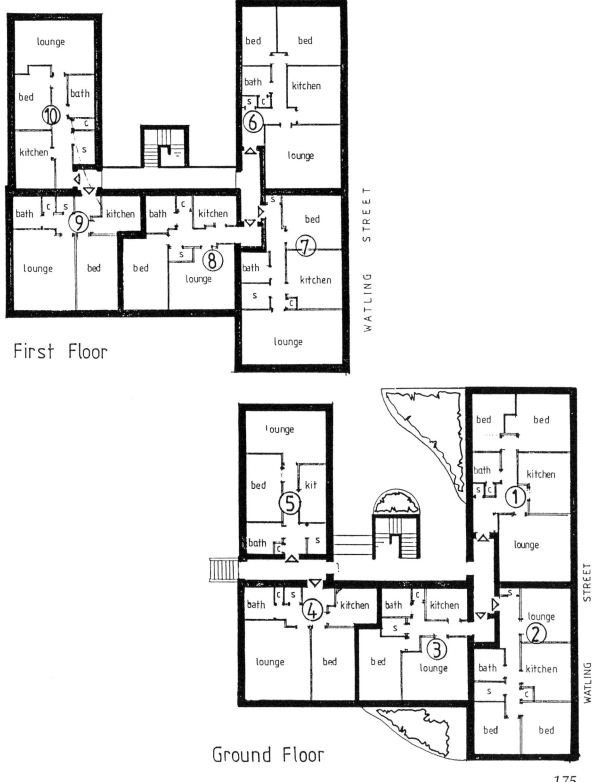

First Floor

Ground Floor

WEST

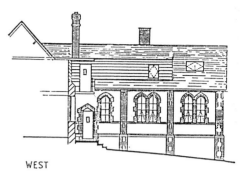

WEST

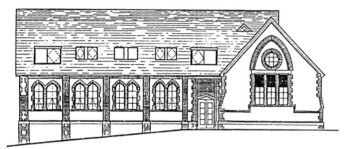

NORTH

RIGHT *View from the east, showing inserted dormers.*

walls to form bulkheads just above window head level. These false ceilings have also probably helped to improve sound insulation between the flats. Only in one case was it felt necessary to lower the ground-floor window cill level. It was also necessary to provide natural lighting to the first-floor flats, since there were no windows at this level in the original building. This has been done by inserting roof lights in the outer, more prominent roof slopes, and dormer windows in the slopes less visible from the road. Aesthetically this is not ideal, the large, rather boxy dormers breaking the roof lines rather unhappily, but the problem was not an easy one, as the upper floor volumes were not large enough to permit the use of the less obtrusive inset dormers. New ceilings have been inserted in the first-floor rooms, partly hiding the trusses but reducing heat loss. Roof insulation has also been provided. The new first floors are of timber joist construction and most of the new partitions are non-loadbearing, apart from some solid party walls.

Most of the replanning was carried out within the existing structure, removing most of the lower and later outbuildings. The main addition was that of a staircase tower in the space between the two parallel wings, with an open gallery at first-floor level giving access to the upper flats. The alternative would have been a series of internal staircases in each section, with consequent loss of floor

176

EAST

EAST

SOUTH

177

space. The scheme produced five self-contained flats on each floor, three of one bedroom and two of two bedrooms.

As usual with projects of this kind there were a number of structural problems. A well was found in the cellar, on the line of a new loadbearing wall, one roof truss was rotted where it was built into the wall, and on the first floor there were some roof beams at inconvenient levels which had to be modified without affecting the structure as a whole.

The work was financed by a loan from the borough council, and the cost was about £170,000 in 1984/85. The scheme was designed and supervised by the association's in-house architects. In general, this project has been successful, but it does illustrate some of the problems of converting a building of this type for domestic use, where an upper storey cannot be inserted without disturbing the roof line. A conversion into *houses* rather than flats, with some 'gallery' type rooms, might have overcome some of the difficulties, but would probably not have created so many units, and the resultant less conventional design may not have attracted local authority assistance, being perhaps more suited to private sector designs for individual clients. An attractive building, however, and one with strong local associations which would have made its loss regrettable, has been given a new role in the village community.

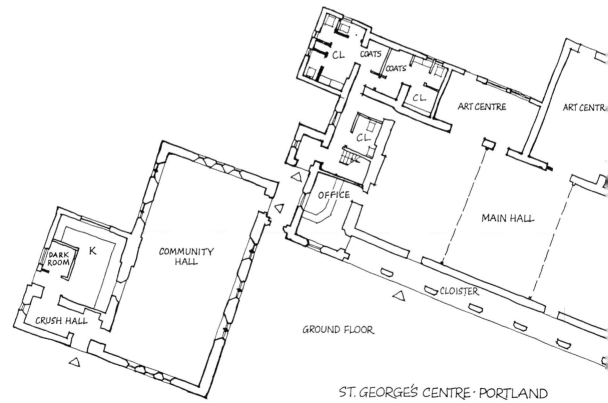

ST. GEORGE'S CENTRE · PORTLAND

Saint George's Centre, Portland, Dorset

This was a typical mid nineteenth-century church school, built in 1857 of the local Portland stone, with a slate roof, in Victorian Tudor style. The original building consisted of a large hall, divided by folding partitions to form classrooms, with an open lean-to cloister along the front, and slightly projecting gabled two-storeyed wings at each end. The left-hand (west) wing contained smaller rooms on each floor, while the right-hand (east) wing comprised the school house. This was extended, with a projecting wing to the right, at a slightly later date, in similar construction. At the rear of the main hall was a lower classroom block, probably of later date, and a range of lean-to lavatories and stores. A second hall or schoolroom was built *c.* 1880, detached from the main building, to its southwest. This was in a Gothic rather than Tudor style, with an open timber roof.

The school continued in use until 1965, when it was replaced by a new building on another site. Although it had been a church school the building reverted to the freeholders, the Crown, in 1979. Its future was then uncertain. It was known that the Crown wished to sell the site and there was a real possibility that the building would be demolished. Although it had been listed Grade II in 1978, Crown property can be demolished without listed building consent, but the local authority have to be consulted. The position was complicated by the fact that the site, although owned by the Crown, was common land.

The threat to the school gave rise to considerable local concern; it was felt that the building should be preserved, both as part of Portland's history and because some people believed that it could

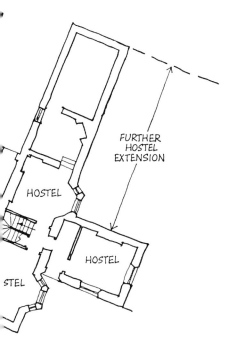

FURTHER
HOSTEL
EXTENSION

HOSTEL

HOSTEL

STEL

179

Institutional buildings: case studies

fulfil a useful new function in the community. A local trust, the Isle of Portland Heritage Trust, was therefore set up to acquire the school and to repair and convert it. The aim was to use the building as a community centre, and as a home for the Royal Manor Workshops, a society of local artists and craftsmen.

From the start there were problems. The Crown at first appeared unwilling to sell to the Trust, possibly hoping to obtain a better price on the open market. Eventually, however, the Crown agreed to sell to the Trust for £25,000, provided that this sum was raised within three months. At this stage the attached school house was not for sale, as there was a sitting tenant. With the help of grants from the county and borough councils the Trust was able to raise the purchase price and acquire the school, early in 1983. Early in 1984 the school house became vacant and was offered for sale on the open market. Since it could have been an embarrassment to the Trust to have another owner on the site, it bought the house at a cost of £21,500.

After having stood empty for several years, the buildings had suffered from neglect and vandalism, and needed a considerable amount of repair. The cost of this was estimated at about £150,000. Grants were obtained from the Historic Buildings and Monuments Commission for England, from the county and borough councils under the Historic Buildings Acts, from the Development Commission for the workshops, and from the Pilgrim Trust and the Ernest Cook Trust (a private charity). A loan was given by the Architec-

Construction of the new rear block in Portland stone.

View from the east.

tural Heritage Fund. Since the buildings are not to be sold, this loan will have to be repaid out of income.

It was decided to carry out the work through the Manpower Services Commission, using local unemployed workers, and the Trust has become an official agency for Manpower Services Commission schemes on Portland. With such schemes, expert supervision is essential, and fortunately a skilled stonemason was found to take charge of this side of the work. In fact, several of the young people employed on the work have since found permanent employment in the stone industry.

As usual in MSC-funded schemes, the Commission has paid the wages of the workers, leaving the Trust to provide the materials. Considerable local support has been given, in the form of gifts of stone and timber, much of it second-hand, and some coming from the prison and former Borstal Institution on the island. Most of the roofs have had to be reslated, and some of the stonework renewed, including features such as window mullions. The bell turret in the centre of the roof of the hall had to be reconstructed, and it was set in place by a helicopter team from the Royal Navy. One rather unusual problem encountered was the discovery of a large underground water cistern, the existence of which had not been known

TILE-HANGING

EXPOSED CONCRETE

Interior of the later hall, under repair.

when the work started. This was surveyed by divers from the Royal Navy before being sealed off. The old lean-to block at the rear of the original hall has been rebuilt, in Portland stone, to provide better accommodation.

A series of craft workshops is being built (1987) in the old playground at the rear of the school, and these will provide permanent local employment. The later hall to the southwest has been repaired and is in use as a community hall, being available for letting for various functions. Part of the main building now houses the Tourist Information Centre. It was considered important to put part of the building into use as soon as possible, while the work was still in progress. Although this has caused some inconvenience it has encouraged public support for the scheme.

The school house is to be extended and converted into a field studies hostel. With its unusual geological, natural history and archaeological features, the Isle of Portland attracts a number of study groups. It is also hoped to use the building to house a new local history archive, and information gathered by the Trust's environmental team in association with the Nature Conservancy Council. This has been a worthwhile local project, making use of a building of character and providing both short-term and long-term employment. The architect was C.F. Davies of Dorchester.

BRICK
IMNEYS

ENTRY

B

LR

ENTRANCE HALL

NORTH ELEVATION

The Convent of Bethany, Boscombe, Bournemouth, Dorset

This building began as an orphanage, founded by the Sisters of Bethany, an Anglican order of nuns whose mother house was at Clerkenwell, London. In 1872 the nuns bought a site in what was then quite a rural area of Boscombe, adjoining the Church of Saint Clement, which was then being built to the designs of J.D. Sedding. For the orphanage Norman Shaw was appointed architect, and he produced an original and distinctive design in the Arts and Crafts style, contrasting with the rather austere Gothic Revival style used for most convent buildings at that time.

The first block to be built, in 1874, was a long rectangular building of three storeys, the top storey being formed in the roof, which was steeply pitched. The ground floor contained the refectory and other communal rooms, the first floor a series of teaching rooms, while the attic contained dormitories lit by ranges of large dormer windows. These, and the windows of the first floor below, were separated by large brick chimney stacks, projecting externally from first-floor level upwards.

What made the building of particular interest was its construction, of in-situ concrete; an early example of the use of this material. On the ground floor this was left exposed, giving an appearance rather like pebbledash, but with the 'lift' lines of the shuttering clearly visible. The upper walls were tile-hung, the tiles being bedded directly on to the concrete. In 1880 a second range was built on the south side of the orphanage block, and at right angles to it, to provide accommodation for the nuns. This was of similar design and

ABOVE *View of the main block. Note the range of chimneys.*
LEFT *The chapel, with the main block visible at the*
rear, and RIGHT *the in-situ concrete walls, showing 'lift' lines.*

construction, but without the projecting chimney stacks. In 1928 a
chapel was added at the south end of this wing, linked back to the
orphanage block at its west end by a single-storey cloister, thus
enclosing a courtyard garden. The architect for the chapel was W.G.
Newton. Like the original building, this was an interesting Arts and
Crafts design, with a range of full-height bay windows in each of the
long walls.

In the later 1930s the orphanage was closed and the buildings
adapted for other uses by the community. Before this work could be
completed, however, it was stopped by the outbreak of war. During
the war the building was hit by a bomb, but the solid concrete
construction stood up well to this, and damage was limited to one
end of the former orphanage block. Repairs were eventually carried
out, this time in conventional brick construction. In 1962 the
community decided to move the mother house from Clerkenwell to
Boscombe, and there were a number of additions in the usual flat-

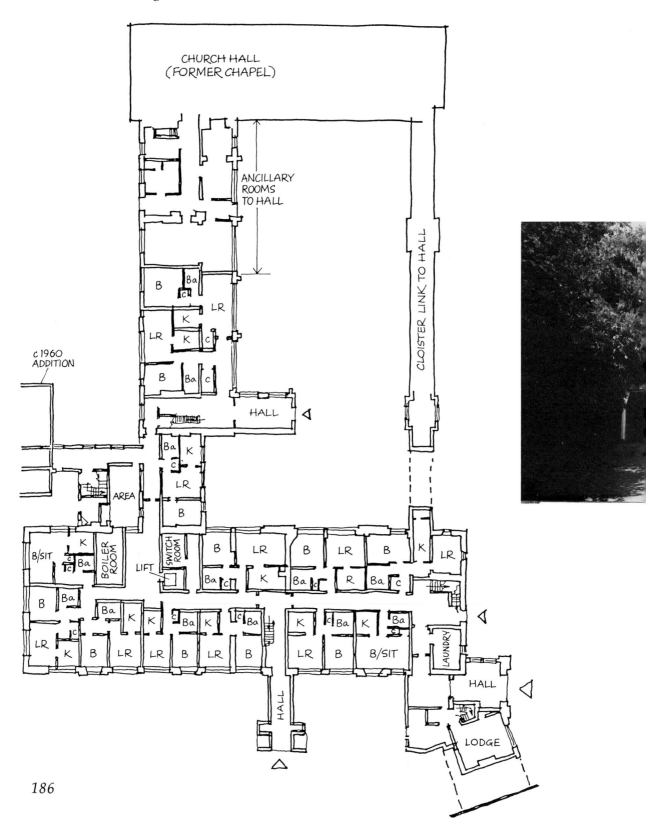

CHURCH HALL
(FORMER CHAPEL)

ANCILLARY
ROOMS
TO HALL

CLOISTER LINK TO HALL

c 1960
ADDITION

B | Ba
c

LR

K

LR | K | c

B | Ba | c

HALL

Ba | K
c

LR

B

AREA

B/SIT | K
c
c | Ba

BOILER ROOM

SWITCH ROOM

LIFT

B | LR | B | LR | B | K | LR

Ba | c | K | Ba | c | R | Ba | c

B | Ba

Ba | K

K | K | c | Ba | K | c | Ba | K | c | Ba | K | Ba

LAUNDRY

LR | K | B | LR | LR | B | LR | B | LR | B | B/SIT

HALL

HALL

LODGE

roofed style of that time. By 1978, however, the community decided to dispose of the buildings and invited the Bournemouth Borough Council to buy the whole site, which was done in 1980.

The convent stood in extensive and well-wooded grounds, and it was decided to develop these for local authority housing, converting the convent buildings into old people's flats, with a warden's accommodation. The development of the site involved the demolition of Saint Clement's church hall, and the former convent chapel was converted by the council into a new church hall, incorporating some rooms in the former nuns' wing which had previously been associated with the chapel.

By this time the whole complex had been listed as a Grade II* building, and the conversion was designed to retain its character and, where possible, to restore original features which had been changed. It was not practicable to remove all the *c.* 1960 additions, and, indeed, it is proposed to convert some of these into additional accommodation. Internally there were few features of interest. Both the orphanage and the nuns' wing had comprised simple, indeed austere, accommodation, and the main value of the building lay in its exterior. The few interior features of interest were preserved; in one of the flats the kitchen is entered through a Gothic arch.

The necessary internal replanning to form the flats, and to comply with the fire regulations, has not therefore caused any real damage to the building. In addition to the warden's flat, forty-five units have been provided for sixty people, comprising nineteen bed-sitting room flats, eleven one-bedroom one-person flats, and fifteen one-bedroom two-person flats. There is also a laundry room, and all the flats have door entry phone systems. All three floors have been used, a new lift having been installed. The flats are planned leading off a central corridor, echoing the original first-floor layout, and all units are self-contained. Some of the rooms had rather high ceilings. False ceilings were inserted in these, both to reduce heating costs and to produce more pleasantly proportioned rooms, but without altering the windows. A certain amount of repair was needed, some problems being caused by the direct bedding of the tile-hanging, but the in-situ concrete has stood up well to a hundred years of weathering.

The architect for the scheme was R.J. Patterson, Dorset County Architect, the project architect being R.J. Pearce. The approximate cost of the work in 1981 was £586,612 (excluding the conversion of the chapel). This compares with the original cost of the orphanage wing, in 1874, of £6,000.

The development of the grounds for housing has inevitably altered the setting of the building, but the new housing has been carefully designed and landscaped, and the former convent is certainly more visible to the public than before.

The main entrance.

188

The Royal Victoria Patriotic Building, Wandsworth Common, London

This large Victorian building is a well known landmark in south London, adjoining Wandsworth Common. It was built in 1856 as an orphanage, for the children of soldiers killed in the Crimean War, with the help of donations from cities and colonies throughout the Empire. The architect was Major Rhode Hawkins, and the design a blend of Gothic and Renaissance styles, apparently emulating a French château. The main building, of three storeys, is planned round two cloistered courtyards, separated by the main hall which is the full height of the building. On the front range there are towers, with truncated pyramidal roofs, flanked by turrets at each end and in the centre, the central tower containing the main entrance and, on its top storey, a large statue of Saint George and the Dragon. There are similar, rather simpler towers in the centres of the side ranges. At the rear is a lower service courtyard, with a second, smaller hall attached to this on its south and, north of the service courtyard, a detached chapel of slightly later date. The building has walls of Suffolk stock brick with stone dressings and slate roofs.

The main hall was used for meals and assemblies, the ground floors of the courtyard ranges for teaching, and the two upper storeys for dormitories. The hall had a handsome open timber roof, with a boarded ceiling painted with the coats of arms of the benefactor authorities. The walls also had stencilled decoration, with the royal arms of Queen Victoria on one end gable. In the courtyard ranges the intermediate floors were formed with wrought iron filler joists, with concrete infilling, an early example of an attempt to provide fireproof floors.

The building remained in use as an orphanage until the First World War, when it became a military hospital. It reverted to its original use after the war, but during the Second World War it was used as an interrogation centre by MI6. In 1947 it was taken over by the London County Council as a school. This use continued until a new school was built on an adjoining site in 1978, when it was left empty and suffered from considerable neglect and vandalism. Lead was stolen from the roofs; gutters and downpipes became blocked; and as a result there was widespread dry rot attack. Nearly all the windows were broken, and interior fittings destroyed or damaged—a depressingly familiar story.

Despite the fact that the building was listed Grade II, the Inner London Education Authority, which had taken over from the London County Council, was not allowed by the terms of its charter to carry out maintenance work on unoccupied buildings. The authority did, however, try to sell the building on the open market,

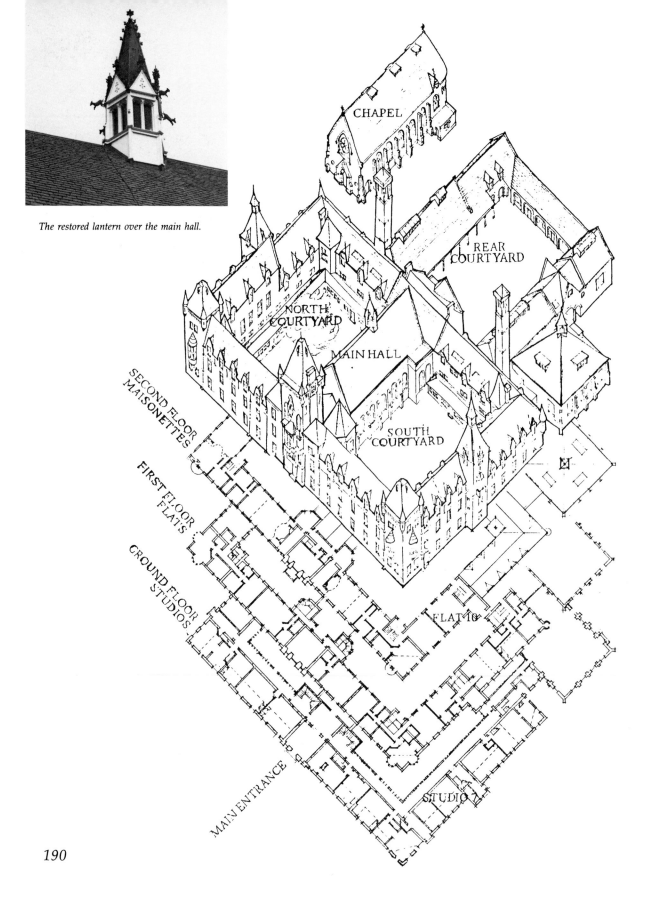

The restored lantern over the main hall.

CHAPEL

REAR COURTYARD

NORTH COURTYARD

MAIN HALL

SOUTH COURTYARD

SECOND FLOOR MAISONETTES

FIRST FLOOR FLATS

GROUND FLOOR STUDIOS

FLAT 10

MAIN ENTRANCE

STUDIO 7

190

but, because of its size and condition, the restrictions placed on its use by the borough council and the additional responsibilities involved in purchasing a listed building in need of much repair, there was little response. Eventually an agreement was reached with the Tuberg Property Company to purchase the whole building for £1, on condition that certain basic protection and separation works were carried out. This company, and its architects, had already restored and converted other problem buildings, and considered that this one could be made financially viable.

A scheme was therefore prepared and agreed with the borough council. This provided for the ground floors of the courtyard ranges to be used as offices, with workshops in the service courtyard, flats and maisonettes on the two upper floors, and the use of the two large halls by a drama and dance school. It was considered essential to retain the character of the building, and to restore those features which had been lost. External alterations were kept to a minimum, and new doors and windows were designed to match those existing. All the external brickwork was cleaned and the stonework restored where necessary. Some of the rooms had very high ceilings and window cill heights. This problem was overcome, both in the flats and the offices, by inserting mezzanine gallery floors, thus gaining extra floor space without altering the windows. On the top floor, which was partly in the roof, some roof lights have had to be inserted, generally in inconspicuous areas. In order to make best use of this roof space the main trusses had to be modified. All the flats have dual outlook, into the courtyard and to the exterior.

ABOVE *The tower above the main entrance, with figure of St George.*

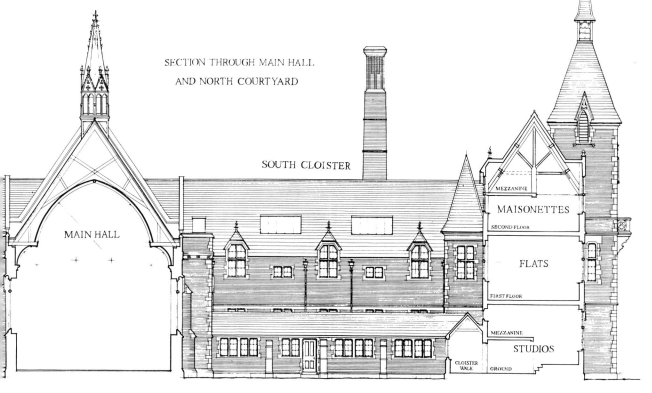

SECTION THROUGH MAIN HALL
AND NORTH COURTYARD

SOUTH CLOISTER

MAIN HALL

MEZZANINE

MAISONETTES

SECOND FLOOR

FLATS

FIRST FLOOR

MEZZANINE

STUDIOS

CLOISTER WALK

GROUND

The restored roof of the main hall.

The provision of adequate means of escape in case of fire presented some problems, particularly in view of the mixed use of the building, but these were overcome by providing staircases to the flats quite separate from the offices. The various officers of the Greater London Council proved very helpful in enabling the work to be done without detriment to the character of the building; the provisions of the *London Building Act*, allowing some discretion to the district surveyor, being in some ways more flexible than the Building Regulations applying to areas outside London. Incidentally, this system is being changed, the Building Regulations applying to the whole of England, but it is to be hoped that the advantages of the London system will not be entirely lost. The use of the two large halls by the drama and dance school has meant that it was not necessary to divide up these rather fine interiors.

One of the original staircases.

Apart from matters of design, there were considerable structural problems. As has been stated, the building was badly affected by dry rot, including the concrete infilling of the upper floors, where some of the old timber shuttering had been left in position and had become infected by the fungus. In addition, just as the sale of the building was being completed the roof of the main hall was destroyed by a fire, which weakened the structure. This meant that priority had to be given to this part of the building. Fortunately it was still covered by the education authority insurance policy, which permitted a full-scale restoration. The original timber-framed roof was replaced by steel trusses of similar design, the ornamental lead-covered fleche in the centre of the roof was restored, and the internal scheme of ceiling decoration reproduced, partly from a photographic record and partly from the remains of the badly charred paintings. This involved a good deal of research, to discover the coats of arms of the various donor authorities, and they have been carefully copied, even incorporating some minor errors in the original designs.

This restoration of the hall was carried out by a general contractor, with specialist sub-contractors, after obtaining tenders in the normal way, but for the rest of the building a different system was adopted, since the scheme had to be almost entirely self-financing. The only grant obtained was one from the Greater London Council for the restoration of certain historical features. As the main source of finance was to be the proceeds from the sale of leases of the flats, these had to be completed in stages, to ensure an adequate cash flow. The owner therefore acted as his own contractor, appointing a project manager who employed and supervised eight directly employed men and the various sub-contractors, with a full-time foreman, and working in close collaboration with the architects, who now occupy one of the office suites. It was necessary to exercise strict control of costs, but at the same time to ensure that the quality of the work was appropriate to the character of the listed building.

As far as the flats were concerned, the purchasers had the options of buying them in three different stages of completion. First, a 'shell' conversion. This covered structural alterations, including construction of mezzanine floors and provision of services, leaving all internal planning and finishes to the purchaser. Second, a partial conversion, including also partitions, doors and maisonette stairs. Third, a full conversion, including all finishes and decorations. The majority of purchasers selected the partial conversion, thus giving themselves more freedom of design.

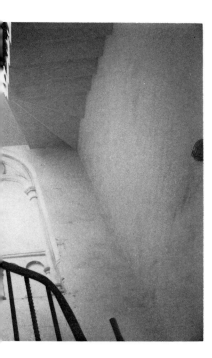

Both the flats and offices have proved popular. The site has a pleasant open aspect adjoining the common, and is conveniently accessible to central London. Purchasers of the flats have included actors, designers, teachers, musicians and entertainers. Tenants of the offices include architects, quantity surveyors, designers, a film location firm and a video casting firm, while tenants of the workshops include a photographer, a piano restorer, and cabinet, model and sign makers.

The detached chapel was sold to another developer and converted to studios. This has resulted in the loss of the interior character, but the exterior has been preserved and it was not considered that any other use for this building was practicable.

This case is particularly interesting in showing how a building which many prospective purchasers would have considered, and indeed did consider, a hopeless case, can be rescued and given a new lease of life in a viable manner. Apart from the Historic Buildings grant from the Greater London Council, the whole scheme has been self-financing. The architects were Dickinson, Quarme and Associates of London. The cost of restoring the hall, largely covered by insurance, was £460,000, including the restoration of the decorations. That of the remainder of the building worked out at £22 per square foot, in 1983. Incidentally, the original building, in 1856, had cost £31,337.

194

10 Churches and chapels

Quite a large number of churches and chapels become available for conversion, having been closed because of population changes. They may be in small villages, where the congregation can no longer afford to maintain the building, and parishes are amalgamated, or in town centres where the resident population has largely moved out to the suburbs. In many cases it will be found that the legal problems arising from conversion proposals will be as great as the structural ones, since the sale of a church can often be subject to restrictive covenants governing its future use.

As far as the Church of England is concerned, the disposal and use of redundant churches is governed by the *Pastoral Measure* of 1968, modified by the *Redundant Churches Act* of 1971, and the amended *Pastoral Measure* of 1983. The first step is the preparation of a pastoral scheme, providing for the church to be made redundant, often as the result of the amalgamation of livings or parishes. The planning authority is asked for its comments on the proposal, but has no power to prevent it. If the scheme is approved by the church authorities, the future of the church building has to be considered by the Church Commissioners, who are first required to consult the Advisory Board for Redundant Churches on the architectural merit of the church. Once a church has been made redundant there are only three alternatives for its future. If it is of real architectural or historic importance, and in particular if the interior and fittings are of so much value that conversion to another use would be damaging, it may be vested in the Redundant Churches Fund. This is a body set up specifically to hold and care for such churches, and it receives finance both from the Church and from the State.

If the building does not qualify for vesting in the Fund, it becomes the duty of the diocesan authorities to try to find a suitable alternative use for it, and this involves full discussions with the local people. If the church is listed, any alterations needed for the new use will need listed building consent. In addition, before approving any new use, the Church Commissioners will consult the Advisory Board for Redundant Churches. Problems which have to be faced in these cases include the treatment of the churchyard and the disposal of monuments and fittings. The question of the churchyard, especially if it has been used for recent burials, can present real problems, as strong local feelings may be aroused. It is no

All Saints Church, Lewes. This redundant church has been converted to an Arts Centre, with minimal external alteration. Even the churchyard path has not been tidied up.

195

exaggeration to say that in many cases there is as much local concern about the graves as about the church itself. If consent is given for any new use, and the church is subsequently sold again, any future proposal for another use will almost certainly require the approval of the Church Commissioners, as well as normal planning permission and listed building consent.

Following the declaration of redundancy, unless the church is to be vested in the Redundant Churches Fund, there is a waiting period of up to three years for a use to be found for the church. At the end of that time, if it has not been vested in the Fund and no acceptable new use has been found for it, the Church Commissioners can order the demolition of the church, even if it is listed, without the need for listed building consent, although if there is opposition from the Advisory Board, the planning authority or certain other sources, a non-statutory public inquiry may be held. In the amended *Pastoral Measure* of 1983, provision is made for a church which has been vested in the Redundant Churches Fund to be taken from the Fund and put to a new use, but such cases are likely to be very rare, and only if the new use is one which will preserve the essential character of the church.

A redundant chapel in Worcester, converted to a discotheque and night club. It would sometimes be difficult to obtain permission for such a change of use, but in this case the fabric has been largely unaltered, and the internal works are reversible.

In the cases of churches and chapels of other denominations, this procedure does not apply, but any sale has to be approved by the appropriate denominational authority, and conditions governing the use of the buildings and the treatment of the churchyard, and of any graves, may be equally strict.

In all cases planning permission will be needed for any change of use, and the requirements of the building, fire and public health regulations will have to be satisfied. Following the recent revision of the Lists of Buildings of Special Architectural or Historic Interest, far more churches and chapels are now listed, and many are now Graded I or II*, which means that the Department of the Environment will have to approve any alterations.

Looking now at the possibilities for conversion, we shall find that most churches and chapels fall into one of two main types. First, we have the traditional Gothic church. This may be a simple building, consisting of nave and chancel, perhaps with a tower, one or more porches, and often an added vestry. It may be a cruciform building, with transepts and perhaps a central tower, or it may have one or two aisles, sometimes with a clerestory lighting the upper part of the nave. Such churches may indeed be medieval, or of nineteenth or twentieth-century date in traditional Gothic style. Second, we have the typical post-Reformation church or chapel, consisting basically of a single 'preaching space', perhaps with a small projecting sanctuary, vestries and a west tower. These buildings often have galleries, with windows in the side walls at the upper and lower levels, giving the appearance externally of a two-storeyed building.

Redundant churches and chapels have been put to many uses, and this is not a new phenomenon. As we have seen in an earlier chapter, after the Reformation many of the monastic churches were converted to houses, or for other purposes. Lacock Abbey and Mottisfont Abbey in Wiltshire, and Buckland Abbey in Devon, are examples of this, and in Norwich the Church of Saint Helen was partly converted into an almshouse. Such conversions were often

ABOVE *and* BELOW *St Helen's Church, Norwich, became an almshouse after the Dissolution. Part of the church remains in use as the almshouse chapel.*

Churches and chapels

A small classical church in the West Country, converted to a house. There have been few alterations, and the building still looks like a church.

RIGHT *This former chapel at Tamworth, a prominent building in the street, is now the town's Arts Centre.*

carried out with little respect for the original building, since the Gothic style was out of fashion. Today, though, if a church of any architectural quality is to be converted, the scheme is expected to preserve the character of the building as far as possible.

In recent times, churches have been converted quite successfully for use as museums, art galleries, heritage centres, theatres and concert halls, community centres, offices, shops, houses and flats. The best schemes are those which retain something of the internal, as well as the external, appearance, with the minimum amount of destruction or alteration of the original structure, and where the alterations are reversible, allowing for the church to be restored to its original form if desired at some future date.

Of the two basic types of church, the post-Reformation 'preaching houses' generally present fewer problems, particularly if they are galleried, with two tiers of windows. With these churches, the walls are generally quite high, with a low-pitched roof and a flat, or shallow segmental ceiling. The insertion of an intermediate floor, often necessary for many uses, need not present too many difficulties. Even so, if the interior is of any quality, it is often desirable to leave part of it open to the roof. If the church is not galleried, but has the typical tall windows in the side walls, it is often best to keep the inserted floor back from the windows, to avoid having to alter these.

199

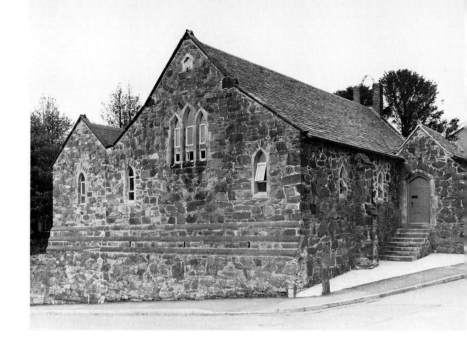

A Roman Catholic church by Pugin, at Shepshed near Loughborough, has been converted as a house and studio with no significant external alterations. It was fortunately not found necessary to insert dormers or roof lights.

The traditional Gothic church can present more difficulties with any conversion scheme which requires the insertion of an intermediate floor. These churches often have a lower eaves level than the post-Reformation type, and steeply pitched roofs. In a simple aisleless church the inserted floor is likely to cut across the existing windows, and the upper storey may have to extend into the roof space. Here the roof trusses can cause an obstruction, and there will be difficulties with lighting the upper storey. A few inserted dormers, if carefully designed, may be acceptable, but too often these are obtrusive, especially if they are of a domestic style. Flush roof lights may sometimes be more appropriate, especially in dark coloured roofs, but too many of these can also spoil the line of the roof. In a church with aisles the inserted floor is often at the level of the capitals of the arcade. If the aisles are much lower than the nave it may be possible to stop the inserted floor on the line of the arcades, leaving the aisles open to the roof, perhaps also leaving some or all of the arches open, creating a galleried effect. If the church has a clerestory, this can serve to light the upper storey. The most difficult churches to convert in this way are those with the nave and aisles of equal height, with separately pitched roofs with valley gutters—a type often found in the West Country and in Kent. Here, lighting an upper storey can be very difficult, but sometimes most of any necessary dormers or roof lights can be inserted in the inner roof slopes, avoiding disturbing the outer roof lines. If the church has a good, well proportioned interior it is an advantage if part at least of the nave can be left open to the roof.

For any public use the fire authority will have to be satisfied about the means of escape, and may well require more exits than existed in the original church. Requirements may be even more stringent if it is desired to obtain a full theatre, or music and dancing licence.

Before a church is sold for conversion, it is likely that most of the movable fittings, pews, pulpit, etc., will have been removed, often for use in other churches. The wall monuments and stained glass windows may, however, have been left in the building, although any medieval or other valuable glass will probably also have gone. Whether these features can remain in position will depend on the new use. For certain public purposes some, or all, of the glass can often remain, but in a domestic conversion this may be less desirable, making the resultant house rather dark. The glass, though, should not be destroyed. Victorian stained glass is now being more appreciated, and if it cannot be used in another church it should be offered to a local museum. As a last resort it may well have some sale value.

The position with monuments is rather similar. For most public uses there is no reason why they should not remain in position. Even in a house, if they have not been removed by the families of those they commemorate, or the church authorities, they may be able to stay. If we accept the view that alterations to a church, particularly to one of any historic or architectural interest, should be reversible, in case future developments enable it to revert to its original use, then it is surely best for the monuments to remain if at all possible. They are, after all, part of its history.

A situation sometimes arises where, although most of the church is converted for a new use, part (generally the chancel) is to remain in use for regular or occasional worship. In other cases the galleries, and perhaps the aisles, may be shut off for other purposes, either as church rooms or to be let as offices or club rooms, leaving the nave and chancel in use. Such schemes need to be carried out very carefully, and there will have to be thorough sound insulation between the different sections. There may also be difficulties with lighting the nave if the aisles or galleries are sealed off, and the church has no clerestory. Such a scheme can, however, sometimes solve the problem of a church which has become too large for its present congregation, by reducing maintenance and heating costs. In other cases the whole church, except possibly for the chancel, may be altered so as to be capable of use for secular purposes during the week, perhaps with a stage or platform at the west end, and movable seating—a return, in effect, to medieval practice.

As we have seen, with any conversion proposals the churchyard can present difficulties, and if any graves have to be disturbed the permission of the Home Office must be obtained.

In recent years there has been a growing appreciation of the importance of the archaeology of churches. Even a Victorian church may have been built over medieval foundations. Since these are likely to be disturbed when a church is altered for a new use, for instance by the laying of a new floor, or drainage work, the planning authority may well make any consent subject to a condition requiring opportunity to be given for archaeological investigation before, or during, the work. The cost of this work, and of any delay it may cause, should be allowed for when preparing estimates for the scheme.

The thirteenth-century guest chapel of the Cistercian Abbey at Coggeshall, Essex, became a barn after the Dissolution. In the early twentieth century it was restored as a Chapel of Ease to the Parish Church, as seen LEFT.

The Old Chapel, Tollard Royal, Wiltshire

This was a small rural Primitive Methodist chapel, built in a simplified Italianate style. The walls were of flint, with brick dressings, and the roof covered with plain tiles. Each of the long walls had three plain tall round-headed windows, which were fitted with sashes. The south gable wall, containing the entrance, was given a more elaborate treatment. The central door, with a semicircular fanlight, was set in a large, shallow, arched recess, also round-headed, which contained above the door an inscribed stone tablet. This was flanked by long windows matching those in the side walls. The gable verge had two oversailing brick courses, with a saw-tooth course below them and, below this again, a projecting stepped brick band course. The verge treatment, without the band course, was repeated round the eaves.

In plan, the chapel was a simple rectangle, without galleries, and was quite small, the internal dimensions being about twenty-six by sixteen feet. The building was not listed, but at the time of its conversion the area had not been resurveyed. The chapel closed in 1977 and was then sold, and used as a store. The then owner considered converting it into a house, but did not proceed with the idea. He did, though, deface the commemorative tablet by dressing back the raised lettering.

The chapel was bought by its present owner in 1982. Many of these little chapels have been converted into houses, all too often losing much of their original character in the process. In this case, though, the scheme, carried out by the architect for a member of his

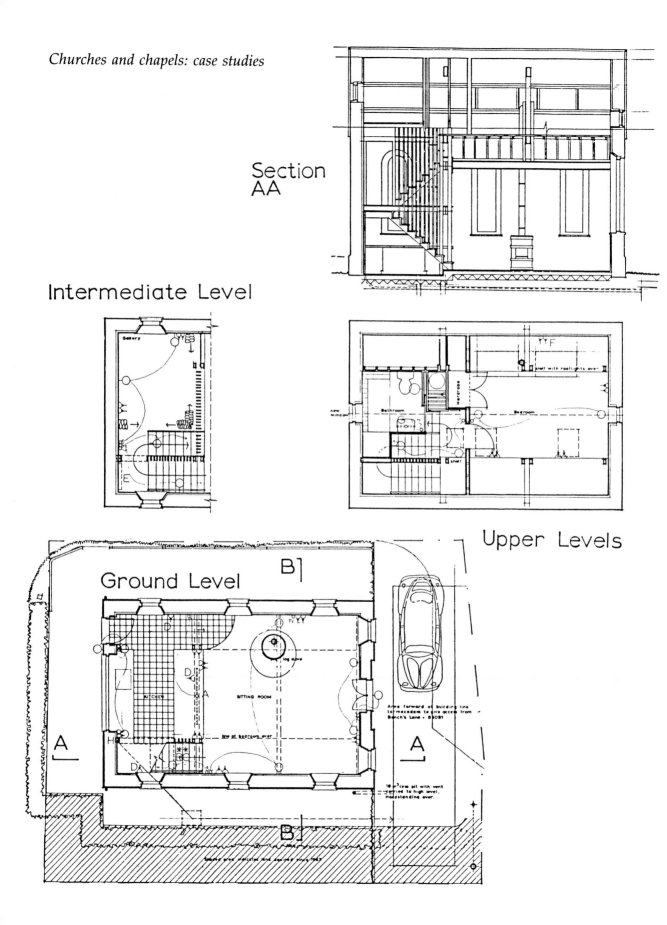

Section
AA

Intermediate Level

Upper Levels

Ground Level

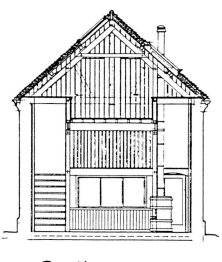

Section
BB

own family, was designed to make the best use of the very small space while retaining something of the feeling of a single-cell building. The internal replanning was governed by the fact that the height to tie-beam level was about thirteen feet, and to the internal ridge about twenty-two feet.

The exterior was largely unaltered except for the insertion of a new door and large window (to light the kitchen area) in the north gable wall, which is not very visible from the road. The stone tablet over the entrance was restored by incising new lettering. Internally the ground floor now consists of a large living room, with a kitchen area in the northern third of the building. A gallery was formed over this, at a height of about six feet six inches from the floor. The kitchen was presumably classed as 'non-habitable' under the Building Regulations, and did not need to comply with the then requirements for minimum ceiling heights, since eased. This gallery is reached by a stair adjoining the west wall, which continues up to give access to a bedroom, with its floor about ten feet above that of the living room. This floor would have cut across the windows in the side walls, so it has been stepped up on each side, forming deep bulkheads in the bedroom. At a slightly higher floor level, a bathroom has been formed above the gallery, leaving a gallery ceiling height of about six feet six inches—the gallery also presumed to be a non-habitable space. Both the bedroom and the bathroom extend into the roof space for its full height. It was necessary to modify the roof trusses to accommodate these rooms, and roof lights have been inserted to light them. All the exposed roof timbers have been treated with a fire-retardant fluid. Heating is

Interior, showing gallery over kitchen area.
The bedroom is on the next level up.

by means of a free-standing solid fuel stove in the living room, with a metal flue pipe, making no pretence at being a domestic chimney and probably similar to the original form of heating in the chapel.

This scheme has produced an attractive small house of, admittedly, unconventional design, without losing the character of the original building. The cost of the work in 1983, excluding the cost of purchase, was about £35,000. The architect was Michael Drury of Saint Anne's Gate Architects, Salisbury.

Interior, looking towards the entrance from under the gallery.

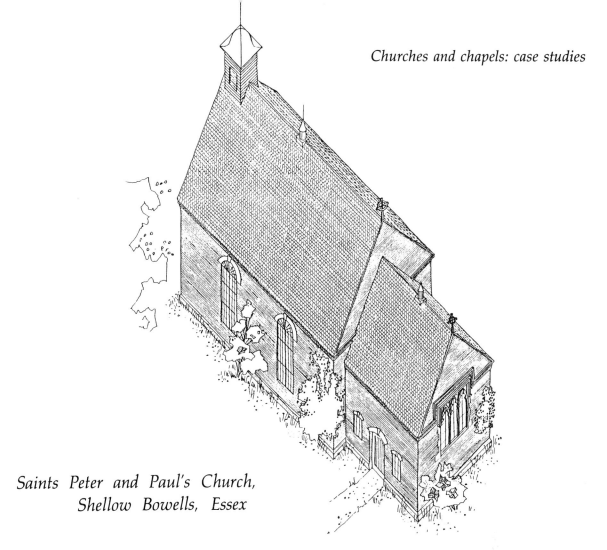

Saints Peter and Paul's Church,
Shellow Bowells, Essex

This small church was built in 1754. It was a simple building, consisting of a nave and rectangular chancel divided by a round-headed chancel arch of classical design, and without aisles or galleries. The walls were of brick, and the roofs tiled, with a weatherboarded timber bell turret at the west end. A brick dentil cornice at the eaves was continued across the east and west gable walls. The main entrance was in the west wall, with a date stone in the gable above, and there was another doorway in the south wall of the chancel. The east and west windows were square-headed, of Gothic design, possibly later alterations. The nave was lit by two tall round-headed windows in the south wall, and there were two similar, blank windows in the north wall. The roof, which incorporated some re-used oak timbers, possibly from a former church on the site, was of king-post construction, concealed behind a flat plaster ceiling, with moulded cornice, forming a substantial roof void.

The church was declared redundant in 1972, and as it was not considered to be of sufficient architectural merit to be vested in the Redundant Churches Fund it became necessary to find an alternative

207

LEFT *View of the former church from the southwest, and* RIGHT *interior, looking east and showing new gallery and spiral stair.*

use for it. After considering various alternatives, it was decided that a domestic-cum-studio conversion would be the best solution to the problem, and the church was bought by the present owner, Mr Thistlethwaite, at the end of 1974. This was one of the first churches in the area to be considered for residential use, and there was some initial opposition to the idea. Following some direct consultations between the Church Commissioners and the planning authority, however, consent was eventually granted for this change of use.

One of the main problems concerned the churchyard. As this contained some graves which might at some date be re-opened and used for burials by the families owning them, the churchyard was not originally included in the sale. All the new owner was able to obtain was a three-foot wide strip of land round the walls of the church, for maintenance purposes. The consequent lack of an adequate curtilage was one of the original planning objections, and the clear space outside the windows, within the site, did not comply with the Building Regulations. Eventually some additional small projecting areas of land adjoining these windows were added to the site, and the owner was also able to buy the path leading from the church, through the churchyard, to the adjoining road. This still left no car parking space, and nowhere to site the cesspool or septic tank. This problem was eventually overcome by the owner having to buy a plot of land on the opposite side of the road, to accommodate a cesspool, with a car parking space above it, the drains being taken down the path from the church across the road. All these problems added to the cost, and difficulty, of the work.

As far as the conversion itself was concerned, the owner was anxious to alter the church as little as possible. The blank windows

Interior, showing the gallery floor.

in the north wall of the nave were opened up, and two segmental-headed windows were inserted in the south wall of the chancel, flanking the existing door. Inside the church, a timber gallery was inserted across the west end, extending along most of the north side, approached by a free-standing iron spiral stair, leaving much of the nave and the whole of the chancel open to the original ceiling level. On the ground floor, a bathroom was inserted under the gallery, in the northwest corner, the rest of the nave becoming a living-studio-workspace area. The chancel became a dining/kitchen, leaving the chancel arch open. Two bedrooms were formed in the northern section of the gallery. The spiral stair was continued up into the roof space, which was not originally altered but has since been converted into a further bedroom, bathroom and store rooms. This meant that the building became, technically, a three-storeyed house, but the normal requirement of the Building Regulations that the staircase in such a situation should be enclosed was not enforced in this case.

A fireplace was inserted in the south wall of the nave, and the chimney from this was carried up into the roof space, finishing with a small metal flue on the ridge, reminiscent of the ventilators often found on such churches. Originally the roof was unaltered externally, but the formation of the rooms in the roof space has resulted in the insertion of some flush roof lights. Also, between the two main stages of the work, the cills of the south nave windows have been lowered and these windows made to open.

Structurally the church was reasonably sound. It was not necessary to retile the roof, but when the new attic rooms were constructed all the existing roof timbers had to be reinforced. This was not so much because there were any real fears about their stability, but because it was not possible to produce, from the engineer's tables, calculations satisfying the Building Regulations in respect of the traditional morticed and tenoned joints of the original construction!

209

Churches and chapels: case studies

The gallery construction is quite independent of the original walls, and most of the alterations are therefore reversible. The internal walls have been plastered, and the original floors (wood block in the nave and tiles in the chancel) have been relaid and made good with matching materials. All the original church furnishings had been removed before the church was sold. There was no stained glass, and the original plain leaded glazing has been retained.

The church was bought for about £5,000. The cost of the first stage of the work, in 1975, was about £10,000, but this included only the floor slab, gallery, drainage and services; all other work, and the subsequent attic conversion, being carried out by the owner. This has been a successful conversion of a small country church. The insertion of the roof lights was perhaps the least happy feature of the scheme, but the desire to make use of the roof space was understandable, and dormers might have looked even more obtrusive. Internally, the feeling of a single open space has been largely retained. It is understood that the owner hopes eventually to buy the rest of the churchyard, and this would certainly make the use more viable. As we have seen, the question of the churchyard, and the future of any graves, is often a major problem when dealing with a redundant church, and this was certainly the case here. The architects were Anthony Richardson and Partners of London.

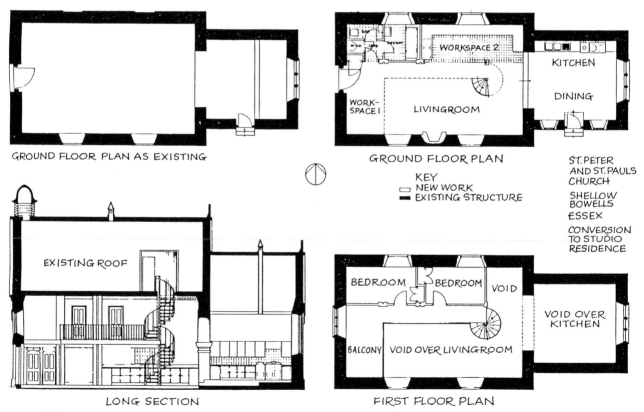

GROUND FLOOR PLAN AS EXISTING

GROUND FLOOR PLAN

KEY
◻ NEW WORK
◼ EXISTING STRUCTURE

ST. PETER AND ST. PAULS CHURCH

SHELLOW BOWELLS

ESSEX

CONVERSION TO STUDIO RESIDENCE

WORKSPACE 2

KITCHEN

DINING

WORK-SPACE 1 | LIVINGROOM

EXISTING ROOF

LONG SECTION

BEDROOM | BEDROOM | VOID

VOID OVER KITCHEN

BALCONY | VOID OVER LIVINGROOM

FIRST FLOOR PLAN

The restored church tower.

Chesil Little Theatre, Winchester, Hampshire

Saint Peter's Church, Chesil, Winchester, was a typical small medieval town church, on a restricted site, with no churchyard and closely surrounded by houses. It was of thirteenth-century origin and consisted of a two-bay nave, a one-bay chancel with no chancel arch, and a south aisle, forming an approximately square plan. South of the aisle was the tower, at its east end. In the nineteenth century a vestry was added, west of the tower and adjoining the aisle. The church was built of a mixture of stone and flint, with some chequer work. The nave and the aisle had separate pitched roofs, tiled, with a central valley gutter. The tower had a tiled pyramid roof, and the belfry walls were tile-hung. Most of the windows were fifteenth-century insertions in the Perpendicular style. Although quite a modest building it had an attractive character, and formed an important feature in the street.

After the Second World War the church ceased to be used, and by 1960 it was becoming structurally unsafe. This was before the passing of the *Pastoral Measure* (see page 195), which established the present procedure for dealing with redundant churches. At that time a church could be demolished by the granting of a faculty, and listing gave no protection.

The Winchester Preservation Trust, which had recently been formed and was concerned about the possible loss of the church, negotiated with the diocesan authorities and was granted a lease of the building, which remains consecrated. In 1960 an agreement was made that the church could be used by the Winchester Dramatic Society, rent free, but with the Society accepting responsibility for all repairs and maintenance. Initially, the Preservation Trust raised funds and carried out repairs and alterations, costing then about £10,000, and in 1966 the church was opened as the Chesil Little Theatre.

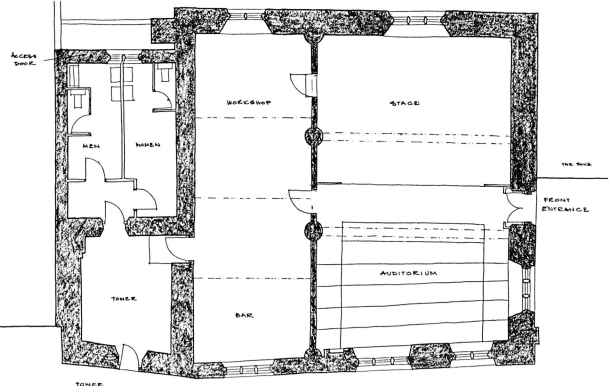

Externally there have been no alterations to the church, but internally the arcade has been built up, partly for structural reasons, as there were fears for its stability. The three-bay nave and chancel have been divided almost equally into the stage and the auditorium, the stage being at the west end and the auditorium, with tiered seating, in the former chancel. The theatre will accommodate about seventy-five people. The aisle contains a bar, green room and a workshop, with storage in the loft above. The vestry was divided to form cloakrooms and dressing rooms, while the tower was used for additional storage. There were no particular problems with the Building and Fire Regulations. As well as the former church entrance in the north wall, leading into a small open courtyard, there was another exit via the tower, and these were considered sufficient.

Since the theatre opened in 1966 there have been further repairs and improvements, costing about £20,000. These included repairs to the roof, installing new heating and stage lighting, and fire precautions works in connection with the granting of a public theatre licence. At the time of writing, further alterations are planned, to re-site the cloakrooms in the base of the tower, freeing the vestry for other uses.

This seems quite a successful solution to the problem of the small town church. The external appearance has been preserved, and although the internal space has been divided by building up the arcade, the alterations seem to be reversible. In fact, the stage, proscenium arch and tiered flooring can all be removed for special events. Since the building remains church property a Faculty is required for any alterations. At the same time, as it is a listed building and no longer used for church purposes, listed building consent is also needed—a rather unusual situation.

The fact that the cost of repairs and improvements carried out since the opening of the theatre has been greater than that of the initial work, is a reminder that if a building is to be put to a new use provision must be made for on-going repairs and maintenance. It is not enough simply to raise funds for the initial repair and conversion work, and hope that the building will require no more attention for a long time. In this case, fortunately, the income generated by the theatre use seems to be adequate for this purpose.

View from the street, showing the constricted site.

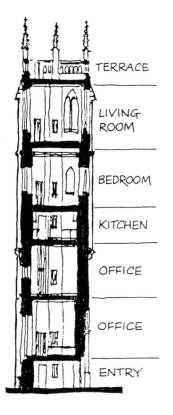

TERRACE

LIVING ROOM

BEDROOM

KITCHEN

OFFICE

OFFICE

ENTRY

Saint Alban's Church Tower, City of London

Saint Alban's Church, Wood Street, was rebuilt by Sir Christopher Wren after the Great Fire of London, in a Gothic style. In 1940 the church was gutted by fire in an air raid, and after the war the body of the church was demolished, leaving only the shell of the tower standing. The City Corporation acquired this, giving an undertaking in 1954 that it would be preserved. In 1959, however, its demolition was considered, in connection with the proposed widening of Wood Street as part of a replanning scheme for the area. This proposal brought protests from several amenity societies and individuals, and in 1961 the City decided to retain the tower on what became an island site in the widened street.

The City Corporation continued to maintain the tower as a monument, and carried out some cleaning and repairs to the stonework over the years. It now stands in the centre of an area of largely post-war development, and it is understood that further redevelopment of its surroundings is planned. In 1985 Messrs Blashford and Peto, a small firm of developers interested in converting old buildings, saw the tower and considered that better use could be made of it. They therefore approached the City Corporation, who agreed to give them a long lease on the building.

The tower was at that time simply a shell; all the interior floors and the roof had been destroyed in the fire, leaving only the outer walls, containing a stone spiral stair. It was decided to convert the tower into an office, with a flat above it. Since the interior of the building was only about twelve feet square, careful planning was necessary to make the best use of the space.

A total of five new intermediate floors have been inserted, not necessarily coinciding with the levels of the original ones. These are of fire-resisting construction. On the ground floor is an entrance hall, with a cloakroom and store. The next two floors form the offices. The third floor, which has no natural lighting, contains the kitchen and bathroom of the flat, the fourth and fifth floors form the bedroom and living room respectively, while a terrace, with fine views over London, has been formed on the roof.

Inevitably with a scheme of this kind there have been a number of problems. At first, the Greater London Council (the fire authority) was not prepared to accept the old spiral stair as a suitable means of escape from the upper floors, and wanted another stair inserted. This would have reduced the already limited floor areas to such an extent as to render the scheme impracticable, and eventually it was agreed

FACING PAGE *The isolated tower in its city setting, on a quiet Sunday morning.*

that the old stair could remain, in conjunction with a sophisticated fire detection and alarm system. On the two office floors, however, lobbies have had to be formed, cutting the stair off from the main rooms.

Since it would be impossible to take furniture up the spiral stair, a large trap door has had to be formed in each floor, just as similar traps would have been inserted for raising bells in the original floors. On the top floor, the living room of the flat, the window cills have been lowered to give a better outlook. To avoid the need for external rainwater pipes, or gargoyles, the roof drainage has been designed to discharge into the main soil stack, which is carried down inside the tower. Externally, the stonework has been repaired as necessary, but the only external alteration has been the aforesaid lowering of the top-stage window cills.

It was expected that the converted tower would be leased on to a private occupant, but in the event it is being taken over by another developer firm, MEPC, who are planning a large-scale reconstruction of the area. It is proposed to make the tower a feature of this scheme.

No grants were obtained for this work. It is an unusual scheme, but the future of the tower is more likely to be secured by using it in this way than by leaving it as a shell, in which state it was an increasing liability, producing no income for maintenance. It is understood that the same developers are planning to carry out a similar scheme at another of Wren's surviving church towers, Saint Mary Somerset. The architects were Frederick Burn, Smith and Partners of London.

FOURTH FLOOR

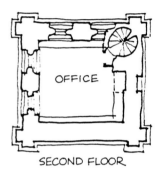

SECOND FLOOR

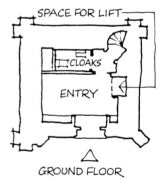

GROUND FLOOR

Interior of the flat kitchen.

216

FIFTH FLOOR

LIVING
ROOM

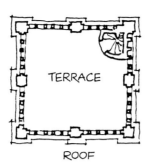

TERRACE

ROOF

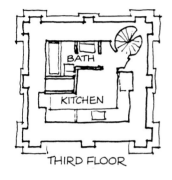

BATH

KITCHEN

THIRD FLOOR

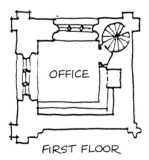

OFFICE

FIRST FLOOR

The roof terrace, and BELOW
*living room of the flat. The
window cills have been
lowered to improve the outlook.*

217

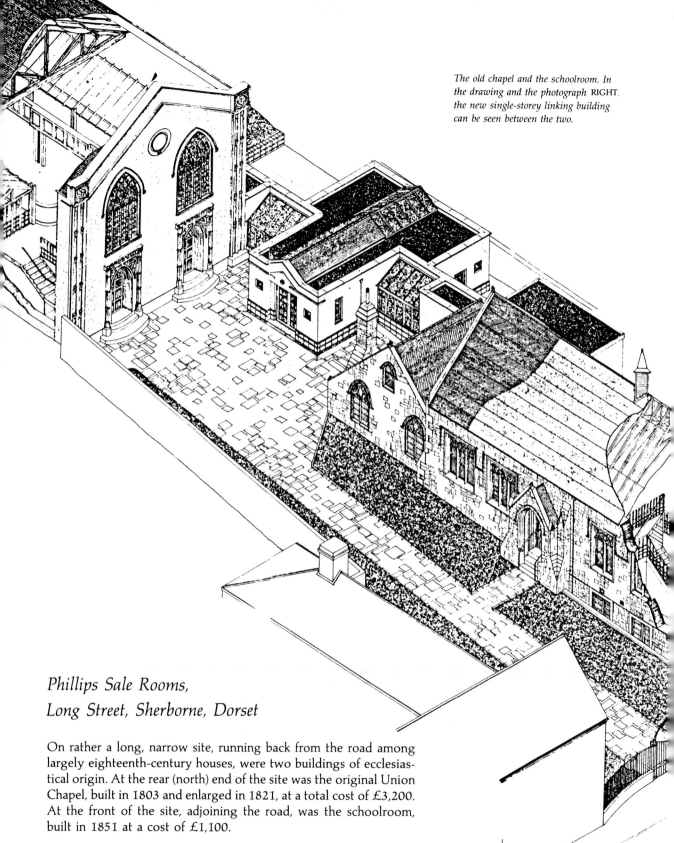

The old chapel and the schoolroom. In the drawing and the photograph RIGHT, *the new single-storey linking building can be seen between the two.*

Phillips Sale Rooms,
Long Street, Sherborne, Dorset

On rather a long, narrow site, running back from the road among largely eighteenth-century houses, were two buildings of ecclesiastical origin. At the rear (north) end of the site was the original Union Chapel, built in 1803 and enlarged in 1821, at a total cost of £3,200. At the front of the site, adjoining the road, was the schoolroom, built in 1851 at a cost of £1,100.

The old chapel was an attractive early Gothic revival building, with plastered walls and a low-pitched slate roof. In the main entrance front were two Gothic style doorways, with pointed arches set in rectangular surrounds with moulded pilasters and carved spandrils, all formed in stucco. Above these were two windows with intersecting tracery, and centrally over these an inscribed circular plaque. Internally, the main chapel building was galleried all round, the galleries having panelled fronts, and the side galleries having been added in 1814. There was a central pulpit near the north end. Attached to this main building on the north was a lower block, roofed at right angles to it, probably a vestry.

The old schoolroom was in a rather later Gothic revival style, with stone walls and a more steeply pitched slate roof. The main block contained one large room, raised over a semi-basement, and entered through a porch on the street frontage at the head of a flight of stone steps. The south wall also contained a second doorway, leading into a small open yard adjoining the porch, and, above the doorways, a large traceried window. In the west, side wall was another entrance and a range of five Gothic style windows. There were no windows in the east wall, which was on the boundary of the site. The main schoolroom had an open timber roof of arch-braced design. At its north end was an attached lower block, partly roofed at right angles to the main block, and partly flat-roofed.

The chapel was closed in 1958, and the buildings were then used without substantial alteration as an auction room and stores. In 1982 they were acquired by the present owners, Messrs Phillips, Auctioneers, who decided to carry out a full conversion, including

the restoration of the old buildings, which were by then listed Grade II. The scheme also provided for a new building, linking the former chapel and the school. Plans were prepared in 1985, and planning permission obtained early in 1986. Work started first on the old school, which was in reasonable structural condition. The old chapel needed more repair, particularly to the ornamental stucco work. In the first stage of the scheme this building has simply been repaired and redecorated externally, leaving any alterations to a later phase of the work.

In the old schoolroom an intermediate first floor has been inserted, just above the level of the window heads in the west wall. This floor is of timber joist construction, carried on steel beams. At the south end of the building a new entrance hall and staircase has been constructed leading to the upper floor. Siting the stair here has allowed the large traceried window in the end wall to be left undisturbed. At the north end, the first floor has been set back, forming an internal well, to avoid disturbing a similar window. The ground floor is used as a saleroom and is entered by the existing doorway in the west wall. Two offices and cloakrooms have been formed in the lower block to the north of the main building. The semi-basement is used as a store. The upper storey has been designed as an office, to be let separately, and is entered from the porch on the street frontage. From this porch the new stairs lead up to the first floor level, lit by the large window previously described. There is a reception area at mezzanine level, leading off the stair. The large window, and the corresponding one at the north end, also help to light the office, but since this has no other natural lighting, roof lights have been inserted in the east roof slope, which is largely hidden from the road. These are the only real external alterations. The old roof trusses have been left exposed, with a plaster ceiling

*Interior of the office, showing the
inserted floor, and roof lights on the left.*

between them. Cloakrooms have been inserted at the north end, as
has a fire escape stair leading on to and over the flat roof of the
lower attached block.

North of the old schoolroom and linking it to the old chapel, a
new block has been built, containing a new main entrance and
reception office for the auctioneers, and two more small offices. This
is a single-storey building, with plastered walls and a partly flat,
partly slated roof with parapets. It has been designed in a simple
modern style to harmonise, and not compete, with the two earlier
buildings, the actual linking corridors being fully glazed.

In the old chapel no external, and few internal, alterations are
planned when it is eventually converted for use as a saleroom. The
galleries are to remain, although their pews will be removed and the
stepped floors lowered. Open timber canopies are to be constructed
over the galleries, and the old pulpit will remain, serving as the
auctioneer's rostrum. The yard to the west of the old schoolroom,
which leads to the old chapel, is to be paved, and the existing iron
entrance gates, dating from 1816, the work of Sprake of Bridport,
will remain.

The adaptation of ecclesiastical buildings for commercial use can
often result in a complete destruction of their character, particularly
when unsympathetic new doors and windows are inserted. Here a
real effort has been made to avoid this, and to accept the limitations
of the existing buildings which occupy an important position in one
of Sherborne's best streets.

The architects were the C.H. Design Partnership of Sherborne,
working with the Anthony Ward Partnership as consulting engi-
neers. The cost of the work to date (1986), i.e. the conversion of the
old schoolroom, basic repairs to the old chapel and construction of
the new link block, was about £130,000, including fees.

Saint Mary's Centre, Lichfield, Staffordshire

Saint Mary's was a large Gothic revival church in the centre of Lichfield, adjoining the market place. It stood on the site of the medieval guild church, but except for the core of the tower nothing remained of the original building. It had been rebuilt on a smaller scale in the eighteenth century, and was again rebuilt in the nineteenth century, to seat a thousand people. The tower was recased and the spire added in 1852, the architect being G.E. Street. The rest of the church was rebuilt in 1868, the architect in this case being James Fowler. It was an imposing building, typical of its period and second only to the cathedral as the dominant feature of the city.

During the present century, though, the congregation steadily shrank. As often happens, the residential population of the city centre was declining and church life tended to centre more on the cathedral, at the expense of Saint Mary's. The high cost of maintenance became an increasing burden on the smaller congregation. This is a common problem with large town centre churches, and has resulted in many of them being closed, and often demolished. By the late 1970s it was realised that if Saint Mary's was to be saved its future use would have to be seriously considered and, fortunately, there appeared to be general local agreement that the church must be preserved. It was not thought desirable for the whole building to pass into secular use, and a rather unusual pastoral

Construction of the new first floor in progress.

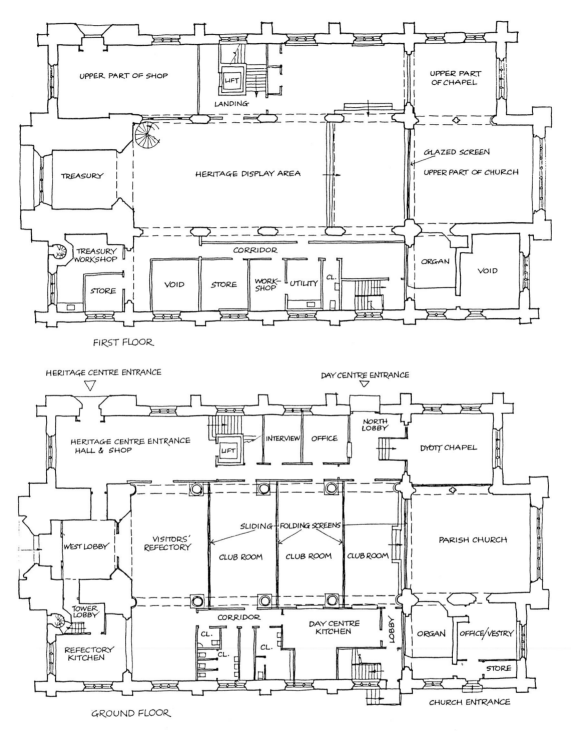

FIRST FLOOR

HERITAGE CENTRE ENTRANCE

DAY CENTRE ENTRANCE

GROUND FLOOR

scheme was devised, declaring the nave, aisles and tower redundant (under the *Pastoral Measure*), while the chancel, sanctuary, Dyott Chapel and vestry remained consecrated. These parts of the church are still used for worship and provide adequate accommodation for the normal congregations.

A trust was set up to take over the redundant sections of the church, and was granted a lease at a peppercorn rent by the diocesan authorities. It was decided that this part of the church should be used for the following purposes: first, a Day Centre should be provided for elderly people; second, space should be provided for a Heritage Centre, with exhibitions and displays illustrating the history of Lichfield, and a Treasury to display the local civic and ecclesiastical plate; and third, a gift shop and a coffee shop should be provided, for visitors to the centre.

In order to accommodate these uses it was necessary to insert an intermediate floor throughout the church, except for those parts still in use for worship. Main steel beams spanning across the church supported lattice girders which carried timber joists and flooring, at the level of the capitals of the nave arcade. Partitions were built up as necessary to suit the new layout, those in the upper storey being mainly in the form of screens, so that much of the original roof structure and the arches of the arcades remain visible. Natural lighting at this level is provided by the original clerestory windows. Although the new floor cuts across the aisle windows it has been kept back from them, and they have not been altered except for one in the north wall. Most of the stained glass has been left in position. The Day Centre, gift shop and coffee shop are on the lower floor, and the Heritage Centre and Treasury on the upper floor. As well as a new stair leading to the upper storey, a lift has been provided for elderly or disabled people. The layout on the ground floor has been so designed as to make it possible for parts to be opened up to the 'church' area when required, to seat 250 people.

New glazed entrance doors have been fitted in the north porch, which forms the main entrance, while a new entrance to the Day Centre has been formed, cutting into one of the north aisle windows near the east end. These are the only external alterations. It would appear that the internal alterations are reversible. None of the original structure has been destroyed, and it would be possible for the interior to be restored to its original form if this were ever required. The Centre, which opened in 1981, seems popular both with residents and visitors, and the whole project has proved an imaginative solution to the problem of the large and under-used town church.

The architects were Hinton Brown, Langstone of Warwick. The cost of the work in 1981 was £330,000. Grants and donations were given by the Lichfield Conduit Lands Trust (the successors of the original medieval church guild), the county and district councils, the Staffordshire Regiment, the Diocesan Board of Finance, and various private trusts and individuals. Income for the maintenance of the building now comes from membership fees for the Day Centre, admission charges for the Heritage Centre, and takings from the gift and coffee shops.

The main entrance with new doors.

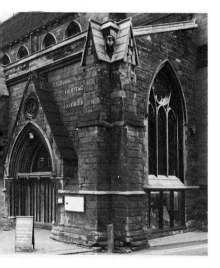

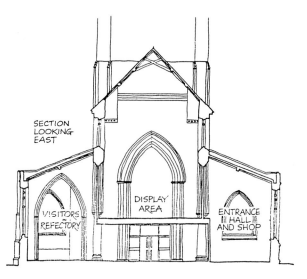

SECTION
LOOKING
EAST

VISITORS
REFECTORY

DISPLAY
AREA

ENTRANCE
HALL
AND SHOP

Saint James' Church, Myatts Park, London

This church was built in 1860, the architect being George Low. It was built to serve the Minet Estate, a mid nineteenth-century development by a family of Huguenot descent, which was planned round a small park, a former market garden known as Myatts Fields. Several of the estate's buildings have finials in the form of cats, a reminder of the original owner's name. Saint James' Church was a typical Victorian Gothic revival building, of coursed rubble stone, with steeply pitched slate roofs. It consisted of a nave of four bays, with aisles and clerestory, a polygonal apsidal chancel, and shallow transepts, rather unusually overlapping the junction of the nave and the chancel. At the (liturgical) west end of the north aisle, and projecting from it, was a tower with an octagonal stone spire. The church was not included in the original Statutory List of Buildings of Special Architectural or Historic Interest for the area, and was not perhaps of outstanding architectural merit, but it was an important local landmark, the spire being a particularly prominent feature.

In 1979 the church was declared redundant, due to an amalgamation of parishes, and at first the Church Commissioners proposed to demolish it. This was opposed by the Minet Conservation Association, a group of local residents who were supported in this by the borough council. In 1980 the church was listed, and the area surrounding the park designated as a Conservation Area. For a time the church was used as a television studio. During this period all the fittings were removed, and while the church stood empty there was some damage due to vandalism—a familiar story.

In 1982 the Church Commissioners sold the church for £50,000 to the Black Roof Housing Co-operative, a registered housing association, for conversion into housing for homeless people from the area. The Society for Co-operative Dwellings acted as development agents. The conversion involved installing two new intermediate floors within the church, one just above the capitals of the nave arcade, and the other at about eaves level. The interior has been completely sub-divided, new solid party and cross walls

View from side road, showing roof lights.

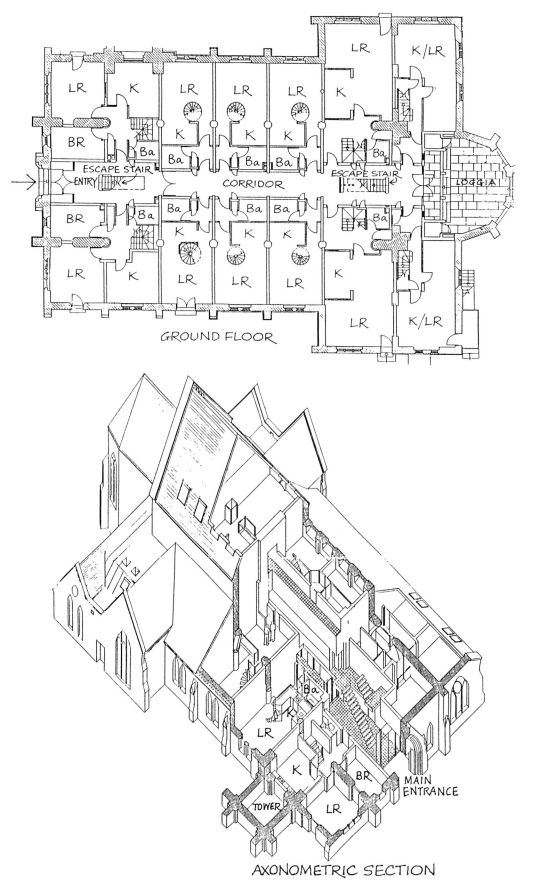

GROUND FLOOR

LR   K

LR   LR   LR   K   LR   K/LR

BR

K   K   K

Ba

ESCAPE STAIR

Ba   Ba   Ba

ESCAPE STAIR

Ba

ENTRY

CORRIDOR

LOGGIA

BR

Ba

Ba   Ba   Ba   Ba

Ba

LR   K

K   K   K

K

LR   LR   LR   K

LR   K/LR

Ba

K

LR

BR

MAIN ENTRANCE

TOWER   LR

227

AXONOMETRIC SECTION

having been inserted to carry the new floors. Externally, however, there have been few alterations, except for the lowering of some of the window cills to suit the new floor levels, and the insertion of roof lights to serve the top floor. All the stained glass has been removed, and the windows reglazed in plain glass to improve the daylighting. Even so, it was necessary to obtain some relaxations of the regulations to avoid having to enlarge the original openings.

The church has been divided into eighteen self-contained maisonettes, with a common room formed at first-floor level in the original chancel. On the ground floor, this chancel was converted into a covered loggia, by inserting pointed-arched openings in the walls. The maisonettes, which vary in size, are planned to open off a corridor which occupies the central part of the original nave, the maisonettes extending into the aisles and some being planned on the ground and first floors, some on the first and second floors. Each maisonette has its own internal staircase, but, to comply with the fire regulations, they also have access on to the main corridors from their upper floors, the corridors having additional staircases at each end. Incidentally, the conversion was carried out under the London Building Acts, which, as we have seen elsewhere, can prove rather more flexible than would have been the case under the Building Regulations, which now apply to London. Care has been taken to provide good sound insulation between the maisonettes, particularly important in a conversion of this type. Heating and hot water have been centrally provided.

The main roof trusses have been left in position where they occurred within rooms. Where, however, they would have been on the lines of party walls they were removed and the walls carried up

ABOVE *New internal common stairs and landing, and* BELOW *common room formed in the upper part of the former chancel.*

to the underside of the roof, this being done to improve the fire resistance of these walls. Problems would have arisen had the trusses been left in position, and the timber subsequently shrunk.

Structurally the building was in reasonable condition. The roofs have been reslated and insulated, and some pointing and repair have been carried out to the external stonework. On the tower some of the buttresses had moved away from the main structure, and have been stitched back to the brick backing with stainless steel rods.

Throughout the whole contract there has been close co-operation between the architects and their clients, with regular site meetings. The maisonettes have been let at a weekly fair rent, and there is a scheme for the maintenance of the communal areas, with a part-time caretaker. Most of the funding for the scheme was from a loan from the Housing Corporation, but there were Section 10 Grants from the Historic Buildings and Monuments Commission for England, grants from the Greater London Council under its Inner City Partnership scheme, and from the Tudor Trust, a private charity. The approximate cost of the work in 1985 was £95,000.

This is a very interesting scheme, securing the preservation of an important local landmark, and providing much needed housing for rent in an inner London area. The interior has been much altered, and although most of the original structure has been retained the work could not be considered reversible; the new floors and walls having been solidly bonded into the existing structure. In this case, though, the preservation of the exterior of the church, in its setting, was the most important consideration. The repair of the tower and spire, a prominent townscape feature, was particularly praiseworthy. The project architect was Giles Pebody of London.

One of the maisonettes. Note the spiral stair and gallery, and exposed arch of the arcade.

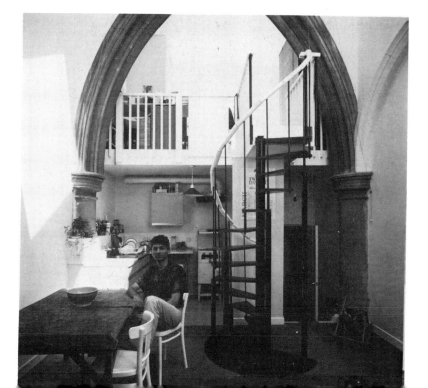

11 Hotels and Inns

At first sight it might seem strange to be considering new uses for hotels and inns when we have seen other types of building being converted to these uses. There are times, though, when a hotel, guest house or inn is no longer viable. In towns, for instance, the character of an area may change from residential to industrial, or an increase of traffic noise and disturbance may be brought about by a new road scheme, making a hotel less popular. Some older town hotels had little or no available parking space—a matter of relative unimportance when they were first built, but a distinct disadvantage today. Others were originally sited near the railway station, and have found their trade declining with that of rail traffic. In yet other cases the hotel's trade will be expanding, and the lack of available space for expansion and improvement of its facilities may result in the owners' deciding to move to a more suitable site and put up a completely new building.

In recent years, too, more and more hotels and inns have been bought by large breweries, and have fallen victim to schemes of reorganisation. Sometimes, when such buildings are sold this is subject to a condition forbidding their reopening as hotels or inns by the new owners. Following changes in patterns of holiday-making, a number of hotels, especially by the sea and in other tourist areas, have been converted to self-catering holiday flats. This does not usually present many design problems, as the requirements of the Building and Fire Regulations are likely to be similar for both uses. It must be remembered, though, that many hotels and guest houses were not originally built as such; they were country or town houses, and it is possible that the regulations will have become more stringent since the original conversion. A further change of use to flats may necessitate improving the fire-resistance and sound insulation of dividing walls and floors, and the protection of staircases, as with other types of building being converted into flats. It may also be found that the requirements for car parking space will be higher when a hotel is converted into self-catering units.

Other possible uses for larger urban hotels are normal residential flats, or offices, perhaps with shops on the ground floor. These buildings are often in a Gothic or Queen Anne style, and may have quite an imposing entrance hall and a fine staircase. Where possible, this feature should be retained in the new scheme, but the Building

A former hotel in Stirling, Scotland, is now the Information Centre for the castle.

The Hopyard Hotel, Worcester, converted to flats by the local authority. A fine Edwardian building, its demolition would have been a loss to the town. Shops have been formed in the central courtyard, seen BELOW RIGHT , and the original staircases have been preserved RIGHT.

and Fire Regulations may make it difficult to keep the open staircase. It may be worthwhile applying for a relaxation of the regulations in appropriate cases.

As well as the larger nineteenth-century hotels, often built as a result of railway expansion, we may find the older, eighteenth-century coaching inns becoming available for conversion, often for similar reasons. These may also be adapted as flats, offices, etc., perhaps combined with shops. In appropriate circumstances they could also become museums or interpretation centres. In many cases these buildings were originally planned round an open courtyard, which may have been roofed over, or partially infilled with later buildings. It will often be possible, and desirable, to restore the open courtyard, both to regain something of the building's original character, and to provide more light and ventilation to the rooms in the centre. Some of the earlier inns of this type actually had open galleries, giving access to the rooms on the upper floors. It may be possible to restore these, but if this is not possible they can perhaps be enclosed largely with glass, recreating something of the original galleried effect. These inns generally had a range of stables, grooms' accommodation and other outbuildings at the rear. These can often be used to provide garaging and other service rooms, and if anything of their original character has survived it should be retained, together with such features as early cobbled, brick or stone paving in the yards.

Hotels and inns

Some of these coaching inns may indeed be earlier buildings, of fifteenth, sixteenth or seventeenth-century date, possibly of monastic or other ecclesiastical origin, which were partly remodelled in the coaching era of the eighteenth and early nineteenth centuries. Before any conversion plans are prepared it will be important to carry out a careful historical survey, to avoid the risk of destroying original work. Inevitably in these cases problems arise over the extent of any 'restoration' to be carried out. A timber-framed building may have been plastered, or clad externally in brick or stone, with sashes replacing the original mullioned windows. Internally, early panelling, painted plaster and beamed ceilings may have been plastered over to create a Georgian room. In the nineteenth century the original ground-floor windows may well have been replaced by large plate-glass windows, perhaps with engraved glass decoration. Should the original forms be restored in these cases? Each building will have to be carefully considered, on its merits, but as a general rule it is probably best to do too little, rather than too much 'restoration' of this type, as distinct from necessary repairs. This is especially true if the later work is good of its kind, and conjectural restoration is best avoided. It is all too easy to give the building a 'bogus' period character. Indeed, in the recent past, many old hotels and inns still in use for their original purpose have suffered from this kind of treatment, with fake 'old beams' being inserted in positions where they can have no structural significance.

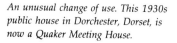

An unusual change of use. This 1930s public house in Dorchester, Dorset, is now a Quaker Meeting House.

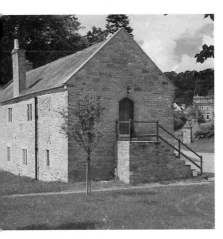

The former Church House at Crowcombe, Somerset. After the Reformation it was converted to houses, but has now been restored as the church hall.

Turning now to the small country inns, many of which have been closed in recent years, we must remember that some of these may originally have been private houses, and there is generally little difficulty in adapting them back for that purpose. Some of the older inns were first built as church houses, where, in pre-Reformation times, the church ales were brewed and sold by the churchwardens. As with the older town inns, the conversion should be carefully handled to avoid destroying original work. At the same time it is often desirable to remove the fake beams and other bogus features which may have been introduced during the later years of the building's use as an inn.

Another group of inns which become available for conversion comprises the mainly nineteenth-century urban taverns and public houses, usually non-residential. They may be converted into shops or offices, and should present few problems. Where, however, they retain decorative features such as engraved glass windows and bar divisions, mahogany counters and seating, and even ornamental plaster ceilings, these should not be destroyed. If it is not possible to retain these features in the converted building, they should first be offered to a local museum for preservation as a whole, rather than being sold off in separate lots. So much of this work has been lost in recent years that it now has a scarcity value, and these town taverns, particularly their interiors, are only just beginning to be appreciated, after so many have been destroyed.

Many old hotels and inns will have spacious cellars. Not only may they have potential for conversion, but they often contain large numbers of old bottles, vats, and other relics of the building's past. Also, some old inns brewed their own beer and there may be the remains of old brewery equipment in an outbuilding. Sometimes, depending on the new use, it will be possible to retain these relics, but if they are not required they should be offered to a local museum, which, incidentally, may be able to help with their dating.

Anyone planning the conversion of an old inn will probably want to learn something of its history. If the inn has been owned by a large brewery the company may have some records, but these do not always go back very far. Research in the local record office may produce early licensing records, or their predecessors the Alehouse Recognizances, giving information about successive licensees. It must be remembered, though, that hotels and inns sometimes change their names during their history—perhaps commemorating a new monarch, or some local celebrity. This is quite an interesting field for research, and, together with a careful historical survey of the building itself, may enable the development of the inn to be discovered and recorded before any alterations are planned.

The nineteenth-century Church Institute at Leeds has been converted into a shopping centre.

Conclusion

To sum up, I think that there are four points normally vital to the success of a conversion scheme.

First, if a building is in poor repair and the cost of the work likely to be high, it is essential to be able to buy it at a reasonable cost. Some owners, seeing the popularity of conversion schemes, including the advantages when it comes to applying for planning permission, get an inflated idea of the value of the building, and hold out for excessively high prices, deterring possible purchasers and increasing the risk of vandalism and general decay. Local authorities have the power in these cases to serve a repairs notice on a listed building which is being neglected and, if necessary, to acquire it by compulsory purchase at the district valuer's valuation—generally lower than the price being asked. So far only a relatively small number of authorities have made use of these powers, but often the threat of action is sufficient to persuade an owner to sell at a more reasonable figure.

Next, and this is related to the last point, it is important not to allow a building to stand empty or neglected for a long period while protracted negotiations take place on its future. The consequent deterioration will increase the eventual cost of the work, and may result in a scheme ceasing to be viable. Many good buildings have been lost in this way. Here again the local authorities can take action. They have the power to move into an unoccupied listed building, carry out essential first aid repairs, and claim the cost from the owner. It is to be hoped that more of them will do this.

Then, particularly if the work is to be carried out by a trust or other voluntary body, it is important to commission a realistic feasibility study before deciding to take on a building. The Community Projects Fund (see Chapter 4, Department of the Environment) may be able to assist in the cost of such a study.

Finally, when it is decided to go ahead, there should be some flexibility over the actual contract arrangements. While the normal lump sum contract may be the most appropriate in the majority of cases, there are others where the work is best carried out at measured rates, or by some direct labour arrangement. All this brings me back to a point made earlier, the need for skilled professional advice when carrying out any but the simplest and most straightforward conversion schemes.

BELOW *At Cheltenham, one of the Regency Pump Houses (forerunner of the one in Pitville Gardens) is now a bank.*

Appendix I

Society for the Protection of Ancient Buildings, policy for conversion of farm buildings

'As a first principle this Society will always argue for the retention of agricultural use for barns and farm buildings. This may require conversion but obviously the alterations necessary within farming use will be considerably less than for many other changes of use. Increasingly farmers are discovering the practical advantages of a traditionally built farm building, of stone or brick, timber-framed or weatherboarded, over many of the cheap modern replacements. The SPAB therefore is only endorsing what many farmers have already done to provide at least part of their storage and working space needs.

If retention of a barn can only be ensured by change of use, then the SPAB considers that certain classes of conversion are more suitable than others—essentially those which respect the scale, space and architectural character of the building in question. The more subdivision, additions (in terms of doors, windows, chimneys, flues, etc.) and alterations necessary for the function of the building in its new guise, the less the original building has been respected, or, indeed, survives.

If we take the principal traditional building on the arable farm, the threshing barn, it has certain architectural and spatial features which any kind of conversion should respect. These include the roof sweep and pitch, the simplicity of the exterior and the few openings, apart from the cart entrances and porches, the quality of the traditional materials and, often, the timber-framed internal structure.

While recognising that every case has its own peculiarities, the SPAB considers certain guidelines, necessarily broadly stated here, should be borne in mind.

First, the type of conversion. Industrial premises, whether ware-housing or light manufacturing, are less likely to interrupt the form of the building. Such uses are more compatible with the spatial qualities and functional character of a barn—even when the requirements of the Building Regulations have been taken into account.

Similarly, farm shops require flexible use of space, and existing entrance points (such as double height doors on threshing barns) are frequently adequate both for delivery and access by the public. Recreational and amenity buildings, such as sports halls or village or community centres, are suitable uses for the same reasons. Often a small internal structure can be added, for kitchen or lavatories, leaving the rest of the space without partitioning or flooring-over. Sometimes dual-purpose conversion can be the answer. Perhaps a small office content with a community centre; an arts or recreational use as well as a commercial one. Nevertheless, there is no doubt that one category is far more in demand than others, and that is conversion to domestic use. Here there is urgent need for strict guidelines, for many so-called barn conversions are literally newly built houses which have merely gained planning consent because of the precedent set by the existing building. As a rule of thumb, the SPAB suggests the following lines are followed.

It is always preferable that the conversion be to a single house, rather than sub-divided into a pair, or more, of cottages. This helps to ensure a minimum of full-height partitioning.

External materials Adherence to the original roof and walling materials, colouring and texture. Care in pointing stonework unobtrusively, using timber without garish varnish or loss of natural finishes, tile, slate or thatch in authentic materials.

External features Doors: principal entrance to reflect original entry point where possible, since this will make sense of the architectural features of the building as it stands. Simple, functional in form and materials. Windows: following the same principle, keeping existing apertures and maximising those as far as possible. In a barn with loading doors, the alteration of solid wood to glass can often be a discreet way of enormously increasing the level of light internally. Roof lights are an option only as a last resort, while dormers are almost always fussy (glazing the gable or gable end can often do the same job, but again much more discreetly). Further new windows should be regarded as a last resort and handled with enormous care, both in terms of where they are placed and how they are designed. Simplicity is a good first principle.

Chimneys If possible, metal flues which are self-evidently functional.

Internal features Roof timbers: any irreversible cutting into or truncation of roof trusses or ties to be avoided. Exposed, the roof is an architectural feature which can be made much of. If part of the space can be left full height, the integrity of the structure is greatly enhanced. Partitions, floors, staircases: if added, their nature should be clearly stated—they are modern additions and could be dismantled if, at a later date, the building was to revert to a use other than domestic. It is always preferable that new floors be inserted on new internal structures and partitions be kept away from the main frame. This ensures that the original structure remains intact and that the work is reversible. Colour-washed walls, an element of irregularity (as opposed to sharp-cornered plasterwork) and a feeling of the original textures will all enhance the interior, respecting its past.

Conversion work often runs into Building Regulations hurdles. Obtaining waivers is always worth a try. Nothing destroys the character and simplicity of the barn more completely than an intrusive setting. Fussy fencing, inappropriate planting or hard surfaces, and, above all, ill-conceived garaging can ruin an otherwise careful conversion. The setting of the building has its own value and must be respected, in just the same spirit.

Finally, it is essential to remember that a barn or farm building will never be, unless it is rebuilt and thus destroyed, quite like a purpose-built house. If your purpose in conversion is to build yourself a conventional house, then a barn is not what you need. A good conversion takes the qualities of the building into account and then rethinks it in architectural terms, not as pastiche but as a design, respecting the original and finding its references and inspiration in that original.'

Reproduced by permission of the Society for the Protection of Ancient Buildings (SPAB).

Appendix II

Yorkshire Dales National Park, policy guidelines for Bunkhouse Barns

'1. The Committee accept that exceptions to the general location criteria on which the Committee's policy for the conversion of barns and other redundant buildings for residential use (as subsequently extended to relate to conversions of such buildings to any form of habitable use) is based, may be made in respect of conversions of redundant farm buildings to form simple bunkhouse accommodation, given that:

(i) The *building* (a) is sufficiently large to accommodate the proposed use without the need for extension or alteration to the roof lines.

(b) is structurally sound and capable of conversion without the need for any substantial rebuilding of the external walls.

(c) is surplus to the requirements of the owner and occupier, and its conversion will not give rise to a requirement for a replacement building.

(d) is of traditional local design and materials, and makes a significant beneficial contribution to the local scene.

(e) is situated on, or in close proximity to, public rights of way which form part of established and well-used long distance routes in areas where similar basic and inexpensive overnight accommodation is considered by the

National Park Authority to be inadequate to satisfy the proven and reasonable needs of the users of such routes.

(f) has existing access adequate to facilitate servicing by the operators and relevant public utilities.

(ii)   The *conversion* could be achieved in a manner acceptable to the National Park Authority, and in particular without:

(a) external alterations materially affecting the character and/or appearance of the building as it exists.

(b) the provision of additional above-ground services.

(c) the formation of new, or improvement of existing, vehicular access.

(d) resulting in a material increase of vehicular traffic on narrow lanes.

(iii)   The *use* is capable of effective control and management by the operators who farm or otherwise control the land which surrounds the building, and whose permanent residence is so located as to facilitate regular supervision by them.

2. Any planning permission granted should:

(a) be based on the submission of detailed plans and such other information as is necessary to judge the various matters itemised in (i) above.

(b) initially be for a temporary period, the length of which shall have regard to the need for the applicant to recoup his initial financial outlay.

(c) be subject to the applicant being prepared, without compensation, to enter into an agreement under S52 of the *Town and Country Planning Act* 1971 with the National Park Authority, to provide such further safeguards as the National Park Authority might consider necessary.'

Reproduced by permission of the Yorkshire Dales National Park Authority.

Appendix III

List of organisations offering advice and/or financial assistance for conversion schemes.

Architectural Heritage Fund, 17 Carlton House Terrace, London SW1Y 5AW
A charity administered by the Civic Trust (see below), which provides short-term capital to help building preservation trusts acquire, restore and resell or let threatened historic buildings.

Building Conservation Trust, Apt 39, Hampton Court Palace, East Molesey, Surrey KT8 9BS
This Trust maintains a permanent exhibition showing some of the problems of building repair and maintenance, and recommended repair methods.

Civic Trust, 17 Carlton House Terrace, London SW1Y 5AW
This Trust is concerned with all aspects of civic design; advises and co-ordinates the work of affiliated local civic and amenity societies; maintains a register of affiliated building preservation trusts, and has drawn up a model constitution. The Trust prepares and issues books, exhibitions and films; has advised the Department of the Environment on the drafting of conservation legislation; gives awards for good design, including work on buildings, many of these being for conversion schemes; and administers the Urban Initiatives Grants Scheme for the Department of the Environment.

Council for Small Industries in Rural Areas (CoSIRA), 141 Castle Street, Salisbury, Wiltshire
The Council provides training in various crafts, and may assist craftsmen in setting up in business in rural areas. It also administers the Development Commission's scheme for assisting the conversion of rural buildings to provide local employment.

Countryside Commission (England and Wales), John Dower House, Crescent Place, Cheltenham, Gloucestershire GL50 3LA

Countryside Commission for Scotland, Battleby, Redgorton, Perth PH1 3EW
These Commissions are concerned with all aspects of the conservation and enhancement of landscape beauty and amenity in the countryside, and the provision and improvement of facilities for its enjoyment. They may give grants for providing interpretative facilities, including the conversion of suitable existing buildings for this purpose.

Department of the Environment, 25 Savile Row, London W1X 2BT
The Department prepares and issues the Statutory Lists of Buildings of Special Architectural or Historic Interest. It determines certain applications for listed building consent, i.e. all applications involving demolition, those for work to Grade I and Grade II* buildings, and those to all buildings which have received central government assistance.

The Department may offer assistance towards the conversion of buildings, irrespective of their historic or architectural interest, in certain areas, to provide employment or assist urban regeneration. It may also, in conjunction with the Royal Institute of British Architects and the Civic Trust (see below and above), assist towards the cost of preparing feasibility studies into restoration or conversion schemes by voluntary bodies.

In Scotland and Wales these functions are carried out by the Scottish and Welsh Offices respectively.

Department of Trade and Industry, 66-74 Victoria Street, London SW1E 6SJ
This Department may give grants for converting buildings for industrial use in regional development areas.

Development Commission, 11 Cowley Street, London SW1P
This Commission finances schemes for converting redundant rural buildings for commercial, industrial and workshop uses in priority areas in England. The schemes are administered by the Council for Small Industries in Rural Areas (see above). The Development Commission may also give grants to help convert buildings in rural development areas into village halls.

In Scotland and Wales these functions are carried out by the Scottish Development Commission, the Welsh Development Commission and Mid-Wales Development.

European Economic Community (EEC), Robert Gregoire, Rue de la Loi 200, 104A Brussels, Belgium
The Community may make grants for cultural purposes, including restoration of historic buildings in town centres.

Georgian Group, 37 Spital Square, London E1 6DY
Originally a sub-committee of the Society for the Protection of Ancient Buildings (see below), this is now a separate body doing similar work in respect of eighteenth-century buildings.

Historic Buildings and Monuments Commission for England, 23 Savile Row, London W1X 2HE

Historic Buildings and Monuments Department of Scotland, 3-11 Melville Street, Edinburgh EH3 7RN

Historic Buildings Council for Wales, Brunel House, 2 Fitzalan Road, Cardiff CF2 1UY

Historic Monuments and Buildings Branch, Department of the Environment for Northern Ireland, Calvert House, 23 Castle Place, Belfast BT1 1FY

These bodies advise the Treasury on the giving of financial assistance for the repair of historic buildings. Normally only Grade I and Grade II* buildings are eligible for assistance, but other historic buildings may receive it under town schemes, or as part of an overall scheme of enhancement in a conservation area. These bodies also advise the Department of the Environment, the Welsh and Scottish Offices, and the Department of the Environment for Northern Ireland on the criteria for listing buildings. The Historic Buildings and Monuments Commission for England has taken over the historic buildings functions of the former Greater London Council, including the administration of financial aid for historic buildings in London.

Housing Corporation, 149 Tottenham Court Road, London W1P 0BN
The Housing Corporation may give financial assistance, by grant or loan, to registered housing associations. This can include conversion of non-residential buildings for housing.

Landmark Trust, Shottesbrooke, Maidenhead, Berkshire
This is a charity which aims to save smaller historic buildings by acquiring them and repairing them. Most of this Trust's properties are let as holiday accommodation, and include some very sensitive and imaginative conversions of non-residential buildings for this purpose.

Manpower Services Commission now renamed *The Training Commission, Moorfoot, Sheffield, South Yorkshire*
This Commission exists to promote employment, and runs short-term schemes to provide temporary employment for unemployed people. These schemes can include conversion of buildings for community purposes.

National Heritage Memorial Fund, Church House, Great Smith Street, London SW1
This fund was set up by parliament in 1980 to make grants or loans to eligible recipients, to assist them to acquire, maintain or preserve land, buildings or other objects which in the opinion of the trustees are of outstanding scenic, historic, aesthetic, architectural or scientific interest. Eligible recipients can be museums, galleries, trusts, amenity societies and similar non profit-making bodies, or the Department of the Environment, but not normally private individuals.

Royal Institute of British Architects, 66 Portland Place, London W1N 4AD
The RIBA is the principal professional organisation for architects. It operates a clients' advisory service, and can recommend architects in different parts of the country with experience in converting buildings. The Royal Institute also administers the Community Projects Fund, providing assistance to community and voluntary groups, towards the cost of feasibility studies into building projects, including restoration and conversion schemes.

Society for the Protection of Ancient Buildings, 37 Spital Square, London E1 6DY
The SPAB provides technical advice on repairs and alterations to historic buildings, organises conferences and courses on this subject, and awards an annual scholarship. It may advise on sources of financial help, and issues (to its members only) periodic lists of threatened historic buildings for sale or lease. The Society's Wind and Watermill Section can provide advice on the restoration of mills and their machinery.

Sports Council, 16 Upper Woburn Place, London WC1H 0QP
This Council exists to promote sports facilities, and may give grants or loans for converting suitable buildings for this purpose.

Tourist boards:

The English Tourist Board, Thames Tower, Blacks Road, Hammersmith, London W6 9EL

The Scottish Tourist Board, 23 Ravelston Terrace, Edinburgh EH4 3EU

The Welsh Tourist Board, Brunel House, 2 Fitzalan Road, Cardiff CF2 1UY
The tourist boards exist to promote tourism in many forms, and may give grants or loans to assist the conversion of buildings for various tourist purposes.

Victorian Society
Originally a sub-committee of the Society for the Protection of Ancient Buildings (see above), this society is now a separate body doing similar work in respect of Victorian and Edwardian buildings.

Local authorities
The structure plans prepared by county councils, and the local plans prepared by district councils, will often include policy statements on the conversion of existing buildings; for instance, conversion of redundant farm buildings into dwellings, holiday units or craft workshops. These should be consulted before making a planning application. Many councils also issue design guides, giving advice on alterations to old buildings. Schemes complying with these are more likely to gain approval.

Local authorities may give assistance towards the cost of repairing and converting old buildings.

The Lists of Buildings of Special Architectural or Historic Interest, compiled by the Department of the Environment, may be inspected at county and district council offices.

Appendix IV *Glossary*

Aisled barn A barn which is divided into three aisles by timber posts supporting the roof, rather like the nave and aisles of a church.

Ashlar stone Stone cut into smooth rectangular blocks and laid with fine joints in regular courses.

Balusters Vertical stone or timber members, often turned, supporting a handrail or capping, as on a staircase or balustrade.

Bay The space between two roof trusses, or between the truss and the end wall of a building or room, or the space between two pillars in the nave arcade of a church.

Bottle kiln A bottle-shaped kiln, usually of brick, found in the older potteries and glassworks.

Bulkhead A section of ceiling raised above the general level, and usually projecting above the floor of the room above, to clear a window head or to provide more headroom over a staircase.

Byre A building to house animals, either a separate building or the lower end of a long-house (see below).

Catslide roof The roof of a lean-to addition to a building, carried down as a continuation of the main roof slope.

Chantry An endowment to provide for masses and prayers to be said for the souls of the donor and his family.

Chantry chapel A chapel built for the saying of chantry masses and prayers.

Clerestory A range of high-level windows, generally lighting the nave of a church above the aisle roofs.

Cloister An arcaded covered way, either free-standing or attached to a building.

Cob A primitive form of concrete, made of chalk, mud and chopped straw.

Collar beam A beam connecting a pair of principal rafters (see below) at some distance above their feet.

Colonnade A row of columns supporting the wall or pediment above.

Common rafters Pairs of rafters forming a pitched roof, either supported on purlins and trusses, or framed in a trussed rafter roof.

Conservation Area An area, generally the historic centre of a town or village, designated by the local authority as being of special architectural or historic interest and given certain statutory protection.

Cornice In classical architecture, the top member of the entablature. In domestic building, a moulding at the junction of the wall and ceiling of a room, or a moulding on an external wall at eaves level.

Cross-wall An internal wall in a building, spanning from front to rear, and often load-bearing.

Cross-wing A wing at one end of a building, at right angles to the main range.

Cruciform Cross-shaped, generally referring to the plan of a building.

Curtilage The area of land belonging to a building, such as the garden of a house.

Double-pile plan The plan of a house two rooms deep, under a single-span roof.

Dressings Ornamental features of a building, often in a contrasting material or colour.

Façade The main external elevation of a building.

Faculty An official permission to carry out alterations to an Anglican church, issued by the chancellor of the diocese.

Field barn (or **down barn**) A barn, sometimes incorporating a cottage, built on downland away from the main farm complex. Typical of the late eighteenth and early nineteenth centuries, when downland was enclosed for grazing.

Finial An ornamental feature at the apex of a gable.

Fleche A small turret or spire, generally rising from the ridge of the roof of a building.

Folly A building in a garden or park, designed primarily for effect, with no functional purpose.

Gargoyle A stone spout, often in the form of a grotesque human or animal head, designed to discharge rainwater from a building.

Gazebo A summerhouse or similar garden building.

Glazing bars The bars dividing window sashes into smaller panes.

Ha-ha A sunken ditch, generally dividing a garden from the surrounding parkland, designed to keep animals out of the garden, avoiding the visual intrusion of a wall or fence.

Hall In early houses, the main living area. In later periods, the hall declined in importance and eventually became the entrance vestibule.

Hatches and sluices The means of controlling the flow of water to a mill, the sluice being the water channel and the hatch the gate to this.

Headers The ends of bricks visible in the face of a wall, sometimes burnt to a darker colour than the sides (stretchers). Use was sometimes made of the dark headers to create patterns in the brickwork.

Hipped roof A roof in which the slopes rise from the eaves on all sides of the building (that is, without gables), the hip being the junction between two adjoining slopes.

Housing Association A registered charity set up to provide housing, normally for rent, on a non profit-making basis.

Inset dormer A dormer formed by cutting into the roof slope, rather than projecting from it, thus avoiding any external break in the roof line.

Intumescent paint Paint which has the property of forming an incombustible foam when subjected to heat, thus forming a fire-resistant coating to timber or steel.

Ionic One of the three orders of Greek architecture, the others being Doric and Corinthian.

Joists The smaller of the timber beams carrying a floor or ceiling. In small rooms they may span between walls, but in larger rooms they are carried on main beams.

Joist housings The notches cut into main beams to support joists.

King-post A vertical timber member rising from a tie-beam in a roof to support the ridge.

Laithe-house A later development of the long-house (see below), where the byre or barn, still attached to the house, is not connected to it internally.

Lintol A beam spanning an opening of a doorway, window or a fireplace.

Listed building A building included in the Statutory Lists of Buildings of Special Architectural or Historic Interest.

Long-house An early type of farmhouse, divided into a living area and a byre for animals, usually with opposed doors and sometimes with a through-passage between the sections.

Louvre A horizontal slat inserted at an angle in an unglazed window to prevent the entry of driving rain.

Lucarne *see* **Sack hoist**

Mansard roof A roof having two pitches, that of the upper part of the roof being flatter than the lower slope.

Mezzanine floor A floor at an intermediate level between two main floors, e.g. one leading off a staircase half-landing.

Mill race *or* **Mill stream** An artificial water course, formed by taking water from a river to serve a watermill, and back into the river below the mill.

Mortice A rectangular recess cut in a timber framing member, to take a tenon (see below).

Mullion A vertical member of stone or timber which divides a window into sections, known as lights.

Open-field farming The medieval system of arable farming where two, or more often three, large fields were divided into strips, allocated to the villagers and farmed in common. This was superseded by a system of enclosed fields from the Tudor period onwards, most of the surviving open fields being enclosed by act of parliament in the eighteenth and early nineteenth centuries.

Open hall The hall or living area of a medieval or early Tudor house, open to the roof, and generally extending through two storeys.

Orangery A garden building, with its front walls largely glazed, originally for growing orange trees and later used for other non-hardy or exotic plants.

Palladian A style of classical architecture, based on that of the Italian architect Palladio, 1518-80.

Pantile A single-lap tile with an S-shaped profile.

Parapet A wall extending above a roof, at the eaves, or at a gable.

Parliamentary enclosures *see* **Open-field farming**

Party floor A floor dividing two occupations (e.g. flats) in the same building.

Pediment A shallow, triangular, or occasionally curved, head to a door or window opening, or a shallow pitched gable, generally supported on a colonnade (see above).

Pilaster A half-column fixed against a wall, often flanking a doorway.

Pitch (roof) The angle of the roof slope.

Portico An open porch on a classical styled building, often consisting of a pediment (see above) supported on columns.

Pre-enclosure farming *see* **Open-field farming**

Principal rafters The main rafters in a roof truss, supporting the purlins and ridge piece.

Purlin A principal longitudinal horizontal member in a roof, supporting the common rafters and carried on the principal rafters of the trusses.

Ridge The upper intersection of the main slopes of a roof.

Rubble stone Roughly cut stone in a wall. It may be laid in courses or completely random laid. The joints are thicker than those in ashlar work, and the whole effect coarser and less regular.

Sack hoist A hoist at high level in a mill, barn or granary, consisting of a short projecting beam with a pulley wheel, where sacks of grain were hoisted for entry into the building. Above the hoist is an opening, sometimes in a dormer, known as a lucarne.

Sash window *or* **double-hung sash** A timber window consisting of vertically sliding sashes, operated by counterweights concealed in a boxed frame.

Saw tooth ornament An ornamental course of brickwork, formed by laying the bricks diagonally, at 45° to the face of the wall.

Segmental arch A shallow curved arch, consisting of a segment of a circle.

Single-pile plan The plan of a house one room deep.

Sluices *see* **Hatches and sluices**

Spandril The space between the arch of a doorway and a square frame surrounding it, sometimes filled with carving, and typical of the Tudor style.

Spine wall An internal wall in a building, parallel to the front and back walls, and generally extending the full length of the building.

Splat balusters Balusters (see above) usually of timber, not turned, but cut from a flat board with a profile echoing that of typical turned balusters.

Staddle stones Mushroom-shaped stones used to support a timber-framed granary, to keep it clear of the ground.

Stretchers *see* **Headers**

Stucco A hard plaster, often incorporating mouldings and ornaments in classical or Gothic style, popular in the late eighteenth and nineteenth centuries.

Tenement Originally a legal term for any permanent property. In later times it has come to be used mainly for flats or houses formed by dividing up larger properties, often of a poor standard.

Tenon A projection on a timber member, formed by cutting away the surrounding timber to fit into a mortice (see above). Generally used for joining timbers at right angles to one another.

Tie-beam A beam joining the feet of a pair of principal rafters in a roof truss.

Toll-house A house associated with a toll gate, used for collecting tolls on the turnpike roads in the eighteenth and early nineteenth centuries. Toll-houses are also found alongside canals, where they performed a similar function.

Tripartite (window) A window, generally with sashes, divided into three lights in width by solid or boxed mullions.

Truss A framed structure supporting a roof, consisting of a pair of principal rafters, secured by a tie-beam or collar-beam, supporting purlins which in turn support the common rafters.

Tympanum A shaped, often semi-circular, solid panel above a window or doorway, sometimes recessed, and ornamented.

Vault (i) an underground chamber, also one used for burials.
(ii) an arched ceiling construction of stone or brick, found in some cellars and undercrofts, and on upper floors of some industrial buildings.

Weatherboarding Overlapping timber boards laid horizontally, to clad a wall (generally used externally).

Wheelhouse A circular structure, sometimes free-standing, but more often attached to a barn, to hold a horse engine to work a threshing machine or other early farm machinery.

Yeoman The more prosperous peasant farmer in medieval or Tudor times.

Bibliography

Benson, Evans, Colomb and Jones *The Housing Rehabilitation Handbook* London, 1982.

Briggs, M.S. *Goths and Vandals* London, 1952.

Building Research Station Digests *Sound Insulation of Traditional Dwellings* Nos 102, 103, 1968.

—*Increasing the Fire-resistance of Existing Timber Floors* No. 208, 1977.

—*Sound Insulation of Party Floors* No. 266, 1982.

CAF Publications Ltd *Directory of Grant-making Trusts* Tonbridge, published annually.

Cambridgeshire County Council *Guide to Historic Buildings Law* 1982.

Cantacuzino, S. and S. Brandt *Saving Old Buildings* London, 1981.

Civic Trust *Environmental Directory* London, 1982.

—*Financing the Preservation of Old Buildings* London, 1971.

—*Forming a Building Preservation Trust* London, 1972.

Civic Trust for the Northeast *Guide to Grants and Loans* Durham, 1984.

Council for Small Industries in Rural Areas *Old Buildings, New Opportunities* Salisbury, revised 1987.

Countryside Commission *Bunkhouse Barns, a new use for redundant farm buildings* Manchester, 1980.

—*Camping Barns in the Peak District* Manchester, 1986.

—*Guide to Countryside Interpretation, Part II 'Interpretive Media and Facilities'* H.M.S.O., 1975.

Cunnington, P.M. *Care for Old Houses* Sherborne, 1984.

—*How Old is Your House?* Sherborne, 1988.

Department of the Environment circulars 12/81 and 8/87, H.M.S.O., 1981 and 1987.

—*New Life for Old Buildings* H.M.S.O., 1971.

—*New Life for Old Churches* H.M.S.O., 1978.

Dobby, A. *Conservation and Planning* London, 1978.

Essex County Council *Residential Barn Conversions; supplementary planning guidance* Chelmsford, 1985.

Parnell, A.C./English Heritage. *Legislation and Historic Buildings* London, 1987.

Parnell, A. and D. Ashford *Fire Safety in Historic Buildings* S.P.A.B. technical pamphlet, London.

Society for the Protection of Ancient Buildings *The SPAB Barns Book* London, 1982.

Smith, John *A Critical Bibliography of Building Conservation* London, 1978.

Sports Council *Recreational Use of Church Buildings* London, 1977.

—*Sport for All in Converted Buildings* London, 1975 (Vol.I), 1978 (Vol.II).

Suddards, R.W. *Listed Buildings, the Law and Practice* London, 1982.

Williams, B. *The Under-use of Upper Floors in Historic Town Centres* York, 1978.

Note The Annual Reports of the Advisory Board for Redundant Churches, and the Architectural Heritage Fund, and those of the Civic Trust Award Scheme give many examples of the conversion of old buildings.

Picture credits

All photographs and drawings in this book have been provided by the author, with the exception of the following: Alphabet & Image 50, 73, 79 above; Burford Marlow Carden Partnership 212; Clifford & Partners 204, 205 left; C.H. Design Partnership 129, 218; C.F. Davis 75 both, 76 below, 77; Dickinson Quarn & Associates 190, 191; Dorset County Council Architect 183, 184; East Midlands Housing Association Ltd 175, 176, 177 below; Essex County Council 13 top and bottom; Dennis Flanders 151; Habitat 27; Donald W. Insall & Associates 91, 92 top right; Interface 107; Kent County Council 65; Leonard Manasseh & Partners 52-3 lower; Ben May 104 all; Giles Pebody 227, 228 above, 229; Rackhams of Lichfield 223; Anthony Richardson & Partners 207, 210; J. Sainsbury plc 8; St Anne's Gate Architects 56 all; 205; Colin Westwood 46; Jane Whitton 2-3, 10 both, 15 above, 16, 21 above, 23, 29 both, 38 above and right, 48-9, 52, 55, 59 below, 61 above, 103, 105 top right and bottom, 106, 107 above, 112, 115, 116 above, 117, 119 both, 120 both, 140, 146, 149, 157, 171, 172, 173, 177, 196 below, 199, 200 above, 203, 215, 219, 224-5 below, 232. The author acknowledges the help of Mr D. Hedworth with respect to her photograph of West Mill, Bridport, and of Poole Borough Council regarding her photograph of the Maritime Museum.

Index

Index